Marcion's Evangelion: A New Telling by A.I.

Forth Given

Marcion's Evangelion: A New Telling by A.I.

Copyright © 2026 by Forth Given

All rights reserved. No part of the **Preface, Introduction, Commentaries, or the specific selection and arrangement** of this book may be reproduced or used in any manner without the express written permission of the publisher, except for the use of brief quotations in a book review or scholarly analysis.

AI Disclosure & Note on the Text

This work is a modern reconstruction of the lost Gospel of Marcion (*The Evangelion*). The reconstruction of the biblical text within this volume was generated using Artificial Intelligence models, guided by prompts derived from historical analysis and the extant Pauline corpus.

While the AI-generated text of the *Evangelion* itself is presented here for historical and spiritual study, the **Preface, Methodology, Compilation, and original footnotes are the unique creative work of the author** and are protected under U.S. Copyright Law.

First Edition: March 2026

Hardback ISBN: 979-8-9944458-7-7

Paperback ISBN: 979-8-9944458-0-8

eBook ISBN: 979-8-9944458-1-5

Published by Forth Given

Greensboro, North Carolina

Contact: forthgivenone@gmail.com

"For whom did You shape me?

Who fashioned me?

Wrath and violence, the blow and the blade
oppress me.

I have no protector but You.

Reveal to me, then, a Savior."

— Yasna 29:1

TABLE OF CONTENTS

PREFACE

The history of Christianity, as it has been transmitted for two thousand years, is not a record of events. It is a crime scene.

The standard narrative—accepted by believers and historians alike—tells us that a Jewish rabbi named Jesus walked the earth, gathered disciples, and left behind a brother named James to steward his family, while a later convert named Paul spread his message to the nations. This narrative is a fabrication. It is a calculated "historicization" designed to bury the most dangerous idea in antiquity.

The Immediate Cover-Up

This crime was not a late development; it began the moment Paul's voice fell silent. The earliest so-called "witnesses"—figures like Clement and Ignatius—were not successors; they were the first handlers of the corpse. They quoted a Paul who had already been dressed in the robes of the Law. Therefore, the antiquity of a text is not a guarantee of its truth; it is often merely a measure of how early the evidence was tampered with.

This text is the fruition of a forensic reconstruction. To arrive here, we have utilized the most advanced informational tools available to examine ancient sources—not to harmonize them, but to expose the contradictions. The core realization of this work is that the trajectory of the Spirit is toward Truth and Justice, and that the distinct barriers of the ego must dissolve into universal consciousness. The Alien God, revealed through the Christ of Paul, is a love so radical it transcends the tribal divisions of the material world.

THE PAULINE FOUNDATION: THE TWO VOICES

Paul is not the follower of a movement; he is the creator of the revelation. However, the letters we possess are not the letters he sent. A forensic analysis of the Original Seven Letters reveals a text at war with itself. Two distinct "voices" compete on the page:

The Authentic Voice: Urgent, mystical, and cosmic. This voice speaks of a Christ who descends from "Heaven downward," unrelated to human history. He declares the Law a "curse" and the Flesh a "prison."

The Ecclesiastical Voice: Bureaucratic, legalistic, and harmonizing. This voice interrupts the first to insert creeds, genealogies, and fictitious scenes of submission to Jerusalem (Gal 2:2) to make the Radical Paul appear subservient to the Old Guard.

The Assimilation Necessity

One might ask: If Paul's theology was so dangerous to the establishment, why did they not simply erase him? The answer is that Paul was already the titan of the faith. His churches spanned the Empire. To win the war for the soul of Christianity, the establishment could not destroy the General; they had to capture him. They could not silence the messenger, so they corrupted the message, burying his radical Spirit under layers of bureaucratic Flesh.

Scholars often point to "historical anchors"—like the Aramaic prayer Maranatha, the eucharistic instructions, or greetings to those "in Christ before me"—as proof that Paul was merely a link in a Jewish chain. We reject this. When subjected to rigorous stylistic analysis, these "anchors" reveal themselves as debris from the construction site of Orthodoxy. They are the clumsy grafts of editors desperate to domesticate the Alien God.

The Core Distillation

The thesis of this book is that if you surgically remove these grafts, the Pauline corpus does not collapse; it clarifies. What remains is a startlingly consistent, irreducible core—a set of nineteen distinct assertions that form a complete, self-contained cosmology. This "Distilled Paul" knows no Bethlehem, no Nazareth, and no biological lineage. His Christ is pure Ideology, descending to shatter the cage of the material world.

THE CORRUPTION OF MEMORY: THE ANCHOR OF FLESH AND TIME

This "Alien" theology was existential poison to the religious establishment. It threatened the authority of the Creator God and his earthly representatives. To neutralize Paul's cosmic Christ, the proto-orthodox faction needed to trap Him. They needed to drag the Spirit down into the Flesh.

They achieved this by constructing two primary Anchors:

1. The Anchor of Prophecy (John the Baptist): To bind the Alien Christ to the Creator's timeline, the evangelists—starting with Mark—co-opted the figure of John the Baptist. By retrofitting this independent apocalyptic prophet as a "forerunner," they forced Paul's timeless Christ into a Jewish succession narrative, subordinating Him to the prophets of the Old Testament.

2. The Anchor of Flesh (James): To bind the Alien Christ to biology, they weaponized the figure of James. In the orthodox tradition, James is presented as the biological "brother of the Lord." In our analysis, this is a theological device. The "Judaizers" used James to create a "smoking gun" of humanity. The logic of the trap was simple: If Christ has a brother who keeps the Law, then Christ must be of the Law.

Together, James and John form the chain that binds the Liberator to the earth.

MARCION OF SINOPE AND THE EVANGELION

Marcion of Sinope was not a vandal; he was a restorer. Born in Pontus (modern Türkiye) around 85 CE, he was not a mystic living in a cave, but a wealthy shipowner and a man of logistical precision. When he arrived in Rome in the mid-second century, he did not find a unified Church; he found a disorganized cult drowning in oral traditions and contradictory texts. He was the first to recognize that the new wine of Christ was being poured into the old wineskins of Judaism, and the vessel was bursting.

He was the first to articulate the "Great Severance": that the Creator-God of the Hebrew Bible—a deity of war, jealousy, and tribal law—could not be the Father of the Jesus who preached unconditional mercy. This opposition necessitated a rejection of the Hebrew Bible and the formation of the first closed Christian canon around 140 CE: The Evangelion (The Gospel of the Lord) and The Apostolikon (the ten Pauline letters).

The Myth of the Razor

For centuries, Heresiologists like Tertullian have accused Marcion of taking the Gospel of Luke and "cutting it with a razor." This is the foundational lie of orthodox history. They claim Marcion excised the birth narratives and the references to the Creator.

A forensic audit reveals the opposite. In textual criticism, there is a principle known as Lectio Brevior Potior—"the shorter reading is stronger." When two ancient texts are compared, the shorter, rougher version is almost always the original, while the longer, smoother version is the later expansion.

Marcion did not cut the text; the Orthodox spackled over it. They took his Evangelion—which began starkly with Jesus descending from heaven to Capernaum—and plastered it with two chapters of "Jewish" birth mythology (Luke 1-2) and a genealogy linking Christ to Adam. They did not protect the Gospel from Marcion; they buried Marcion's Gospel under layers of historicizing "flesh" to make it palatable to the Roman authorities and Jewish traditionalists.

THE LUKAN REVISION: A THEFT OF TRUTH

The Book of Acts functions as a forced "peace treaty," falsely depicting Paul as submissive to James to domesticate his radical theology. This literary theft was supported by later interpolations into the works of historians like Flavius Josephus, where phrases were clumsily inserted to transform a Jewish priest into the "brother of Jesus, who was called Christ." These edits served a singular purpose: to force the Cosmic Christ into the timeline of Roman history and Jewish prophecy.

Consider the account of the Council of Jerusalem. In Paul's own sworn testimony (Galatians 2), he refused to yield "even for an hour" to the demands of the legalists. Yet in Acts 15, the Lukan editor depicts a Paul who happily accepts a compromise, agreeing to impose dietary laws on his Gentile converts. These two accounts cannot both be true. One is the raw voice of the witness; the other is the polished minutes of a corporate merger that never happened.

CONCLUSION: THE RESTORATION

To read the Gospel correctly, we must cut the anchor.

This book is an attempt to reverse the obfuscation. We are returning to the Evangelion of Marcion—the gospel as it likely existed before it was mutilated by the editors of the "flesh." We will strip away the birth narratives, the genealogies, and the false deference to the Creator God. We will dismantle the "Jamesian" cage to reveal the Christ that Paul originally preached: the Alien Stranger who came not to fulfill the Law, but to break it.

We do not offer this reconstruction merely as a theological curiosity, but as a spiritual necessity. By dissolving the accretions of the second century, we recover a Christianity that is not a religion of obedience, but a revelation of pure Spirit. We challenge the reader to look directly at the light, without the protective filter of the Old Testament veil.

The history you know is a prison. This text is the key.

CHAPTER I

The Descent to Capernaum

1 In the fifteenth year of the reign of Tiberius Caesar, Pontius Pilate being governor of Judea, Jesus descended into Capernaum, a city in Galilee.

2 And he was teaching them on the Sabbath days.

3 And they were astonished at his doctrine: for his word was with power.

4 And in the synagogue there was a man, who had a spirit of an unclean devil, and cried out with a loud voice,

5 Saying, "Let us alone; what have we to do with thee, thou Jesus? Art thou come to destroy us? I know thee who thou art; the Holy One of God."

6 And Jesus rebuked him, saying, "Hold thy peace, and come out of him." And when the devil had thrown him in the midst, he came out of him, and hurt him not.

7 And they were all amazed, and spake among themselves, saying, "What a word is this! for with authority and power he commandeth the unclean spirits, and they come out."

8 And the fame of him went out into every place of the country round about.

Healings and The Call of Simon

9 And he arose out of the synagogue, and entered into Simon's house. And Simon's wife's mother was taken with a great fever; and they besought him for her.

10 And he stood over her, and rebuked the fever; and it left her: and immediately she arose and ministered unto them.

11 Now when the sun was setting, all they that had any sick with divers diseases brought them unto him; and he laid his hands on every one of them, and healed them.

12 And devils also came out of many, crying out, and saying, "Thou art Christ the Son of God." And he rebuking them suffered them not to speak: for they knew that he was Christ.

13 And when it was day, he departed and went into a desert place: and the people sought him, and came unto him, and stayed him, that he should not depart from them.

14 And he said unto them, "I must preach the kingdom of God to other cities also: for therefore am I sent."

16 And it came to pass, that, as the people pressed upon him to hear the word of God, he stood by the lake of Gennesaret,

17 And saw two ships standing by the lake: but the fishermen were gone out of them, and were washing their nets.

18 And he entered into one of the ships, which was Simon's, and prayed him that he would thrust out a little from the land. And he sat down, and taught the people out of the ship.

19 Now when he had left speaking, he said unto Simon, "Launch out into the deep, and let down your nets for a draught."

20 And Simon answering said unto him, "Master, we have toiled all the night, and have taken nothing: nevertheless at thy word I will let down the net."

21 And when they had this done, they inclosed a great multitude of fishes: and their net brake.

22 When Simon Peter saw it, he fell down at Jesus' knees, saying, "Depart from me; for I am a sinful man, O Lord."

23 And Jesus said unto Simon, "Fear not; from henceforth thou shalt catch men."

24 And when they had brought their ships to land, they forsook all, and followed him.

Chapter I Notes

The Theological Incipit: The Descent (Verse 1) *"In the fifteenth year of the reign of* Tiberius... *Jesus descended into Capernaum."*

- The Missing Genealogy: The Evangelion opens with a deliberate vacuum. There is no nativity, no Mary, no manger, and no baptism by John.
- The Event: The verb is *katerchomai* ("came down"). In Marcionite theology, the Alien God does not participate in biological reproduction (the domain of the Creator). He simply *is*. He bypasses the humiliating process of gestation and birth, appearing fully formed in Capernaum to begin the invasion.
- The Timestamp: The "15th year of Tiberius" (AD 29) is the only history the Alien God acknowledges. Before this date, He was unknown to the world.

The First Confrontation: "Art Thou Come to Destroy Us?" (Verse 5)

- The Recognition: The "Unclean Devil" is the first entity in the universe to recognize Jesus.
- The Question: *"Art thou come to destroy us?"* This is the thesis statement of the Evangelion. The answer is implicitly Yes. Jesus has not come to reform the Creator's world, but to dismantle the power structures ("us") that hold it together—sin, death, and the Law.
- The "Holy One": The demon calls Him *"The Holy One of God."* This is not the "Holy One of Israel" (a title for the Creator), but the "Holy One of the *Other* God" whom the spirits fear.

The Rebuke of the Fever: War on Nature (Verses 9–10) *"And he stood over her, and rebuked the fever."*

- The Personification: Jesus rebukes (*epitimao*) the fever just as He rebuked the demon.

- The Theology: In Marcionism, physical entropy (sickness, decay) is part of the Creator's flawed physics. By "rebuking" the fever, Jesus treats the laws of nature not as neutral realities, but as hostile combatants. He commands the biology of the Creator to release its victim.

The Catch of Fish: "Taking Alive" (Verses 19–24)

- The Metaphor: The Sea represents the Abyss—the chaotic, darkened world of the Demiurge. The Fish are human souls trapped in the depths of matter.
- The Rescue: The "Net" is the Gospel. The miraculous draft of fish is not a blessing of commerce; it is a Rescue Mission.
- "From Henceforth" (Verse 23): Jesus bifurcates Simon's life. "Before" was spent toiling in the Creator's darkness; "After" is spent in the Alien Light.
- "Catch Men" (*Zōgreō*): The Greek *zōgreō* means "to take alive" (used of rescuing POWs or saving from fire). Jesus is not recruiting fishermen to build a religion; He is recruiting rescuers to pull souls "alive" out of the drowning waters of the material world.

Peter's Terror: "Depart from Me" (Verse 22) *"Depart from me; for I am a sinful man, O Lord."*

- The Old Reflex: Peter reacts with the conditioned reflex of a subject of the Creator: Guilt. He assumes that the presence of God means Judgment for sin.
- The New Reflex: Jesus ignores the confession of sin entirely. He does not say, "Thy sins are forgiven" (yet); He says, *"Fear not."* He replaces the Creator's terror with the Father's assurance.

CHAPTER II

The Cleansing of the Leper

1 And it came to pass, when he was in a certain city, behold a man full of leprosy: who seeing Jesus fell on his face, and besought him, saying, "Lord, if thou wilt, thou canst make me clean."

2 And he put forth his hand, and touched him, saying, "I will: be thou clean." And immediately the leprosy departed from him.

3 And he charged him to tell no man: "but go, and shew thyself to the priest, and offer for thy cleansing, that this may be a testimony unto them."

4 But so much the more went there a fame abroad of him: and great multitudes came together to hear, and to be healed by him of their infirmities.

5 And he withdrew himself into the wilderness, and prayed.

Chapter II Notes

The Antithesis of the Creator: Leprosy as Judgment

- The Precedent: In the Old Testament, the Creator frequently uses leprosy as a weapon of judgment (e.g., Miriam in Numbers 12, Uzziah in 2 Chronicles 26). It is the signature mark of the Creator's displeasure.
- The Reversal: By healing the leper, Jesus is not merely performing a medical miracle; He is undoing a divine sentence. The Creator inflicted the wound; the Alien God heals it. This establishes Jesus not as the servant of the Old God, but as His adversary.

The Theological Pivot: The Touch (Verse 2)

- The Violation: The Mosaic Law (Leviticus 13) mandates the strict quarantine of the unclean to protect the community. To touch a leper is to contract impurity.
- The Superiority: Jesus demonstrates an active Holiness that is superior to the Law. He reverses the vector of contagion: instead of the disease infecting Him, His Life infects the disease. He does not fear the Creator's biological weapon.

The Sovereign Will ("I Will")

- The Command: When the leper asks *"If thou wilt,"* Jesus responds with a single word: *"I Will"* (*Thelo*).
- The Immediacy: There is no prayer to heaven, no ritual washing, and no waiting period. The Alien God operates by Will alone, bypassing the elaborate ritual mechanisms ("Works") the Creator established for cleansing.

Textual Restoration: The Excision of Moses (Verse 3)

- The Cut: The canonical phrase *"according as Moses commanded"* is excised.
- The Rationale: Jesus derives no authority from Moses. To cite Moses would be to validate the very system He came to dismantle. He sends the man to the priest not to honor the Law, but to confront it.

The "Testimony Against Them" (Verse 3) *"...for a testimony unto them."*

- The Legal Trap: The Greek *eis martyrion autois* functions as "a testimony *against* them."
- The Deposition: The priest is the only one authorized to declare a man clean. By forcing the priest to examine the healed man, Jesus compels the Creator's agent to officially certify a miracle that the Creator's Law was powerless to effect. The priest unwittingly signs the affidavit of his own system's obsolescence.

The Strategy of Silence (Verse 3) *"And he charged him to tell no man."*

- The Incognito: Why command silence? In Marcionite theology, the Alien God is a Stranger in enemy territory. He does not want to be confused with the Creator's noisy, political Messiah.
- The Stealth: He operates by stealth, liberating souls ("stealing his goods") before the "Rulers of this Age" fully understand who He is. Fame (Verse 4) is a danger because it draws the attention of the Archons before the work is finished.

CHAPTER III

The Paralytic & The Calling of Sinners

1 And it came to pass on a certain day, as he was teaching, that there were Pharisees and doctors of the law sitting by, which were come out of every town of Galilee, and Judaea, and Jerusalem: and the power of the Lord was present to heal them.

2 And, behold, men brought in a bed a man which was taken with a palsy: and they sought means to bring him in, and to lay him before him.

3 And when they could not find by what way they might bring him in because of the multitude, they went upon the housetop, and let him down through the tiling with his couch into the midst before Jesus.

4 And when he saw their faith, he said unto him, "Man, thy sins are forgiven thee."

5 And the scribes and the Pharisees began to reason, saying, "Who is this which speaketh blasphemies? Who can forgive sins, but God alone?"

6 But when Jesus perceived their thoughts, he answering said unto them, "What reason ye in your hearts? Whether is easier, to say, 'Thy sins be forgiven thee'; or to say, 'Rise up and walk'?"

7 "But that ye may know that the Son of man hath power upon earth to forgive sins," (he said unto the sick of the palsy,) "I say unto thee, Arise, and take up thy couch, and go into thine house."

8 And immediately he rose up before them, and took up that whereon he lay, and departed to his own house, glorifying God.

9 And after these things he went forth, and saw a publican, named Levi, sitting at the receipt of custom: and he said unto him, "Follow me."

10 And he left all, rose up, and followed him.

11 And Levi made him a great feast in his own house: and there was a great company of publicans and of others that sat down with them.

12 But their scribes and Pharisees murmured against his disciples, saying, "Why do ye eat and drink with publicans and sinners?"

13 And Jesus answering said unto them, "They that are whole need not a physician; but they that are sick. I came not to call the righteous, but sinners to repentance."

The Parable of the New Wine

14 And they said unto him, "Why do the disciples of John fast often, and make prayers, and likewise the disciples of the Pharisees; but thine eat and drink?"

15 And he said unto them, "Can ye make the children of the bridechamber fast, while the bridegroom is with them? But the days

will come, when the bridegroom shall be taken away from them,
and then shall they fast in those days."

16 And he spake also a parable unto them; "No man putteth a piece
of a new garment upon an old; if otherwise, then both the new
maketh a rent, and the piece that was taken out of the new agreeth
not with the old."

17 "And no man putteth new wine into old bottles; else the new wine
will burst the bottles, and be spilled, and the bottles shall perish."

18 "But new wine must be put into new bottles; and both are
preserved."

Chapter III Notes

The Authority to Forgive: The Temple's Bankruptcy (Verses 4–7) *"Who is this which speaketh blasphemies? Who can forgive sins, but God alone?"*

- The Jurisdiction Clash: The Pharisees are legally correct. In the Old Testament, forgiveness is a specific legal transaction mediated by the Temple priesthood and blood sacrifice. It is the Creator's monopoly.
- The Hostile Takeover: By forgiving the man's sins *outside* the Temple and *without* a sacrifice, Jesus declares the Temple bankrupt. He asserts an authority superior to the Creator.
- The Mechanism: The Creator forgives via Transaction (Payment/Blood). The Alien God forgives via Fiat (Word/Grace). Jesus proves He is a different God—one of pure Mercy—who does not require the "payment" of pain to absolve debt.

The Call of Levi: The Economic Break (Verses 9–11) *"And he left all, rose up, and followed him."*

- The Abandonment: Levi sits at the "receipt of custom"—the intersection of Empire, Money, and Law (the Creator's systems of control).
- The Instant Severance: Levi does not ask permission or settle his accounts. The call of the Alien God effects an immediate, total severance from the Creator's economy. To follow the Stranger, one must walk away from the "Receipts" of the world.

The Physician (Verses 12–13) *"They that are whole need not a physician... I came not to call the righteous."*

- The Diagnosis: The Law acts as a diagnostic tool—it identifies the "sick" (sinners) but possesses no medicine to cure them. It can only condemn.

- The Separation: Jesus draws a hard line. "The Righteous" (those who successfully keep the Creator's Law) are left to their own devices. The Alien God has no business with them. He comes *only* for the failures of the Creator's system. If you are "whole" by the standard of the Law, you are lost to the Gospel.

The Bridegroom and the Fast (Verses 14–15) *"Can ye make the children of the bridechamber fast, while the bridegroom is with them?"*

- The Suspension of Time: The disciples of John (the Prophet of the Creator) fast because they are still in the "Old Time" of mourning and judgment. The presence of the Alien God (The Bridegroom) creates a pocket of eternity—a wedding feast—where the laws of time and mourning are suspended.
- The Violent Removal: *"The days will come, when the bridegroom shall be taken away."* This predicts the Cross not as a sacrifice offered *to* God, but as a violent act *against* God. The Creator's agents will "take away" the Alien Son, returning the world to its mournful state.

The New Garment (Verse 16) *"No man putteth a piece of a new garment* upon *an old."*

- The "Patch" Heresy: This parable argues against the idea that the Gospel is merely a "patch" to fix the holes in Judaism.
- The Tearing: If you try to sew the Alien Spirit (New Cloth) onto the Mosaic Law (Old Garment), the tear becomes worse. The Gospel is not a repair kit for the Creator's religion; it is a replacement. You must throw away the Old Garment entirely.

The New Wine (Verses 17–18) *"No man putteth new wine into old bottles;* else *the new wine will burst the bottles."*

- The Incompatibility: The "Old Bottles" (Judaism/Law) are brittle, rigid, and settled. The "New Wine" (The Spirit) is active, fermenting, and expanding.
- The Explosion: Mixing the two is not just ill-advised; it is dangerous. The Spirit will shatter the structures of the Law. The Marcionite believer must abandon the "Old Skins" (Synagogue/Temple) to preserve the New Wine.

The Rejection of the "Old Taste" (Omitted Verse 39)

- The Cut: The canonical text includes a verse suggesting that those accustomed to the old wine prefer it ("The old is better"). This is excised.
- The Logic: The Marcionite text refuses to validate the preference for the Old Testament. There is no nostalgia for the Law; the Old Wine is dead and flat. The "Goodness" of the Old Testament is a delusion of those who have not tasted the New.

CHAPTER IV

Lord of the Sabbath & The Twelve

1 And it came to pass on the second sabbath after the first, that he went through the corn fields; and his disciples plucked the ears of corn, and did eat, rubbing them in their hands.

2 And certain of the Pharisees said unto them, "Why do ye that which is not lawful to do on the sabbath days?"

3 And Jesus answering them said, "Have ye not read so much as this, what David did, when himself was an hungred, and they which were with him; How he went into the house of God, and did take and eat the shewbread, and gave also to them that were with him; which it is not lawful to eat but for the priests alone?"

4 And he said unto them, "That the Son of man is Lord also of the sabbath."

5 And it came to pass also on another sabbath, that he entered into the synagogue and taught: and there was a man whose right hand was withered.

6 And the scribes and Pharisees watched him, whether he would heal on the sabbath day; that they might find an accusation against him.

7 But he knew their thoughts, and said to the man which had the withered hand, "Rise up, and stand forth in the midst." And he arose and stood forth.

8 Then said Jesus unto them, "I will ask you one thing; Is it lawful on the sabbath days to do good, or to do evil? to save life, or to destroy it?"

9 And looking round about upon them all, he said unto the man, "Stretch forth thy hand." And he did so: and his hand was restored whole as the other.

10 And they were filled with madness; and communed one with another what they might do to Jesus.

11 And it came to pass in those days, that he went out into a mountain to pray, and continued all night in prayer.

12 And when it was day, he called unto him his disciples: and of them he chose twelve, whom also he named apostles;

13 Simon, (whom he also named Peter,) and Andrew his brother, James and John, Philip and Bartholomew, Matthew and Thomas, James the son of Alphaeus, and Simon called Zelotes, And Judas the brother of James, and Judas Iscariot, which also was the traitor.

Chapters IV Notes

Lord of the Sabbath: The Claim of Jurisdiction (Verses 1–5) *"That the Son of man is Lord also of the sabbath."*

- The Supremacy: This is not a request for an exemption; it is a claim of ownership. The Sabbath is the "Sign of the Covenant" between the Creator and Israel (Exodus 31:13). By declaring Himself Lord (*Kyrios*) of the Sabbath, Jesus asserts that He outranks the God who established the Sabbath. He is not subject to the Creator's calendar; He is its Master.
- The Shewbread Precedent: Jesus cites the incident where David ate the "Bread of the Presence"—bread that was legally restricted to the priests alone (Leviticus 24:9).
    - The Logic: Jesus uses the Creator's own "Beloved" (David) to dismantle the Creator's ritual strictures.
    - The Argument: Physical necessity (Hunger/Life) overrides Ritual Law. If David could desecrate the Temple bread to save his men from hunger, the Son of Man can desecrate the Sabbath to save his disciples. The preservation of Life is a higher "Law" than the preservation of the Creator's rituals.

The Withered Hand: The Definition of Evil (Verses 6–10) *"Is it lawful on the* sabbath *days to do good, or to do evil?"*

- The Moral Trap: The Pharisees watch to see if He will heal (Work). Jesus counters by reframing the definition of "Work."
- The Marcionite Checkmate: Jesus forces a binary choice:
    1. Do Good: Heal the man (which breaks the Sabbath).
    2. Do Evil: Do nothing (which keeps the Sabbath).
- The Indictment: Jesus argues that *passive adherence* to the Law when one has the power to heal is equivalent to *doing evil* ("destroying life"). The Law, by forbidding healing, mandates evil. By healing the man, Jesus demonstrates that the Creator's Law is incompatible with the Alien God's Goodness.

The Anti-Sinai: The Mountain and the Twelve (Verses 12–13) *"He went out into a mountain to pray... and when it was day, he called unto him his disciples."*

- The Typology: This is a reversal of the Sinai event.
    - Moses: Went up the mountain and brought down Tablets of Stone (The Law) to bind the people.
    - Jesus: Goes up the mountain and brings down Living Men (The Apostles) to liberate the people.
- The New Israel: Choosing twelve apostles is a deliberate co-opting of the "Twelve Tribes" symbolism. Jesus is forming a new, spiritual Israel that supersedes the physical lineage of the Creator's tribes.

The Traitor (Verse 16) *"Judas Iscariot, which also was the traitor."*

- The Necessity of Betrayal: In Marcionite theology, Judas represents the necessary link back to the Creator's authorities. He is the one disciple who cannot break free from the old system. The "Traitor" is the one who ultimately prefers the Creator's Law to the Alien Grace, handing the Son over to the Archons of this world to be destroyed.

CHAPTER V

The Sermon on the Plain (The Marcionite Ethics)

1 And he came down with them, and stood in the plain, and the company of his disciples, and a great multitude of people out of all Judaea and Jerusalem, and from the sea coast of Tyre and Sidon, which came to hear him, and to be healed of their diseases;

2 And they that were vexed with unclean spirits: and they were healed.

3 And the whole multitude sought to touch him: for there went virtue out of him, and healed them all.

4 And he lifted up his eyes on his disciples, and said, "Blessed be ye poor: for yours is the kingdom of God."

5 "Blessed are ye that hunger now: for ye shall be filled. Blessed are ye that weep now: for ye shall laugh."

6 "Blessed are ye, when men shall hate you, and when they shall separate you from their company, and shall reproach you, and cast out your name as evil, for the Son of man's sake."

7 "Rejoice ye in that day, and leap for joy: for, behold, your reward is great in heaven: for in the like manner did their fathers unto the prophets."

8 "But woe unto you that are rich! for ye have received your consolation."

9 "Woe unto you that are full! for ye shall hunger. Woe unto you that laugh now! for ye shall mourn and weep."

10 "Woe unto you, when all men shall speak well of you! for so did their fathers to the false prophets."

11 "But I say unto you which hear, Love your enemies, do good to them which hate you,"

12 "Bless them that curse you, and pray for them which despitefully use you."

13 "And unto him that smiteth thee on the one cheek offer also the other; and him that taketh away thy cloke forbid not to take thy coat also."

14 "Give to every man that asketh of thee; and of him that taketh away thy goods ask them not again."

15 "And as ye would that men should do to you, do ye also to them likewise."

16 "For if ye love them which love you, what thank have ye? for sinners also love those that love them."

17 "And if ye do good to them which do good to you, what thank have ye? for sinners also do even the same."

18 "And if ye lend to them of whom ye hope to receive, what thank have ye? for sinners also lend to sinners, to receive as much again."

19 "But love ye your enemies, and do good, and lend, hoping for nothing again; and your reward shall be great, and ye shall be the children of the Highest: for he is kind unto the unthankful and to the evil."

20 "Be ye therefore merciful, as your Father also is merciful."

Chapter V Notes

The Marcionite Ethics: The Original Sermon This sequence represents the original, uncorrupted ethical text of the Alien God.

- The Geography of Grace: The *Evangelion* places this sermon on a level "plain" (Verse 1). The Alien God does not thunder from the heights of Sinai to impose laws from above; He descends directly to the level of humanity to liberate them.
- The Orthodox Overwrite (Matthew's Mount): Later Orthodox editors—specifically the author of Matthew—found this un-Jewish geography unacceptable. To force Jesus into the mold of a "New Moses" and bind Him to the Creator's timeline, Matthew relocated this sermon to a "Mount" (mimicking Sinai) and inserted speeches about fulfilling the Law. Matthew's "Sermon on the Mount" is a later historicizing fiction designed to bury the original "Sermon on the Plain."
- The Silence on the Law: In this original text, there is no language of "fulfilling" the Law (e.g., "Think not that I am come to destroy"). The Alien God does not claim to fulfill the Creator's statutes; He simply issues new commands that supersede them entirely.

The Cosmic Reversal: The Blessings and the Woes (Verses 4–10) The Creator God of the Old Testament explicitly promises earthly wealth, full bellies, and military victory as the reward for keeping His Law (Deuteronomy 28). The Alien God systematically curses the beneficiaries of the Creator's system.

- The Blessed: The poor, the hungry, and the weeping are blessed not because poverty is inherently holy, but because they are the rejects and victims of the Demiurge's material hierarchy. They have nothing tying them to this world.

- The Cursed (The Woes): "Woe unto you that are rich!" Jesus curses the very people the Old Testament Law defines as "blessed." To be full, rich, and well-regarded in the Creator's world means you are perfectly attuned to a system of flesh and death. The Alien God pronounces a death sentence on the Creator's economy.

The Great Antithesis: "Love Your Enemies" (Verse 11) Marcion recognized the command to "Love your enemies" as the ultimate proof that the New God is ontologically distinct from the Creator God of the Hebrew Bible.

- The Creator's Way: The Old Testament operates on *Lex Talionis* (Eye for an Eye) and commands the merciless destruction of enemies (e.g., the Canaanites, the Amalekites).
- The Alien God's Way: By commanding love for enemies, Jesus is not refining the Old Law; He is reversing it. This behavior is impossible for the Creator, who is bound by strict, retributive justice. Unconditional love is the exclusive property of the Alien God.

The Abolition of Property and Justice (Verses 13–14) *"Him that taketh away thy cloke* forbid *not to take thy coat also... of him that taketh away thy goods ask them not again."*

- The Dismantling of Law: The Creator's system relies heavily on property rights, restitution, and courts of law (Exodus 22). By commanding His followers to surrender their cloaks and abandon their stolen goods, Jesus effectively abolishes the concept of earthly justice.
- The Detachment: To demand stolen goods back is to acknowledge the value of the material world. The Alien God demands total detachment from the Demiurge's currency. You cannot fight for property without validating the world that produced it.

"Children of the Highest" (Verse 19) The text promises that those who love their enemies will be *"children of the Highest"* (*Hypsistos*).

- The Hierarchy: In Marcionite cosmology, this term is highly specific. It implies a hierarchy of deities: the Creator God is "Great" (a powerful Archon of matter), but the Alien God is the "Highest," situated above the Creator and previously completely unknown to him.
- The Adoption: By practicing radical, illogical forgiveness, the believer proves they share the DNA of the *Highest* God, not the genetic, retributive code of the Creator.

The Theological Distinction: "Merciful" vs. "Perfect" (Verse 20) *"Be ye* therefore *merciful, as your Father also is merciful."*

- The Definition: The defining characteristic of the Good God is Mercy, whereas the defining characteristic of the Creator is Justice (Law/Perfection).
- The Orthodox Edit: The later Matthean editor altered this command to read, "Be ye *perfect*." The original Marcionite text rejects "Perfection" (flawless adherence to a legal code) in favor of "Mercy" (kindness toward the undeserving). One cannot be "Perfect" like the Creator without destroying sinners; one can only be "Merciful" like the Alien Father by saving them.

CHAPTER VI

The Faith of the Gentile & The Resurrection at Nain

1 Now when he had ended all his sayings in the audience of the people, he entered into Capernaum.

2 And a certain centurion's servant, who was dear unto him, was sick, and ready to die.

3 And when he heard of Jesus, he sent unto him the elders of the Jews, beseeching him that he would come and heal his servant.

4 And when they came to Jesus, they besought him instantly, saying, "That he was worthy for whom he should do this: For he loveth our nation, and he hath built us a synagogue."

5 Then Jesus went with them. And when he was now not far from the house, the centurion sent friends to him, saying unto him, "Lord, trouble not thyself: for I am not worthy that thou shouldest enter under my roof: Wherefore neither thought I myself worthy to come unto thee: but say in a word, and my servant shall be healed."

6 "For I also am a man set under authority, having under me soldiers, and I say unto one, 'Go', and he goeth; and to another, 'Come', and he cometh; and to my servant, 'Do this', and he doeth it."

7 When Jesus heard these things, he marvelled at him, and turned him about, and said unto the people that followed him, "I say unto you, I have not found so great faith, no, not in Israel."

8 And they that were sent, returning to the house, found the servant whole that had been sick.

9 And it came to pass the day after, that he went into a city called Nain; and many of his disciples went with him, and much people.

10 Now when he came nigh to the gate of the city, behold, there was a dead man carried out, the only son of his mother, and she was a widow: and much people of the city was with her.

11 And when the Lord saw her, he had compassion on her, and said unto her, "Weep not."

12 And he came and touched the bier: and they that bare him stood still. And he said, "Young man, I say unto thee, Arise."

13 And he that was dead sat up, and began to speak. And he delivered him to his mother.

14 And there came a fear on all: and they glorified God, saying, "That a great prophet is risen up among us"; and, "That God hath visited his people."

Chapters VI Notes

The Faith of the Gentile: Bypassing the Economy of Law (Verses 1–9) This encounter is a masterclass in jurisdictional authority. The Alien God bypasses the entire theological framework of the Creator's chosen people.

- The Transactional Trap: The Jewish elders attempt to "broker" the miracle by appealing to the Creator's economy of works: *"He loveth our nation, and he hath built us a synagogue"* (Verse 4). They believe the power of the Divine can be purchased with stone, mortar, and allegiance to the tribe.
- The Dismissal of Merit: Jesus completely ignores their legalistic logic. He does not heal the servant because the Centurion funded a building for the Creator; He heals the servant because the Centurion recognizes the true nature of the Spirit.
- The Recognition of Jurisdiction: The Centurion understands Jesus not through the lens of Mosaic Law or Messianic prophecy, but through the lens of pure, hierarchical Authority. Just as the Centurion commands soldiers in the physical realm, he recognizes that Jesus is a Supreme Commander operating from a higher, alien jurisdiction. He knows Jesus does not need physical proximity (flesh) or ritual incantation to command the elements.
- The Verdict on Israel: *"I have not found so great faith, no, not in Israel."* This is a cornerstone of Marcionite thought. The Centurion—an uncircumcised Gentile soldier of the occupying Roman army—possesses a spiritual gnosis that "Israel" (the people trapped in the Creator's Law) entirely lacks.

The Violation of Death: The Ambush at Nain (Verses 10–14) This is not merely a miracle of pity; forensically, it is a direct assault on the Demiurge's ultimate enforcement mechanism.

- The Creator's Weapon: In the Old Testament system, Death is the final sentence of the Law ("the wages of sin"). The funeral procession is the ultimate symbol of the Creator's inescapable cycle of biological decay.

- The Ritual Crime: Jesus commits a deliberate violation of the Creator's purity laws. Numbers 19:11 dictates that touching a corpse or a bier makes one ritually unclean for seven days. Jesus touches the bier (Verse 12). In the Creator's system, the Living becomes polluted by the Dead. In the Alien God's system, the Dead are overwritten by the Living. The Defilement does not infect Jesus; His Life infects the corpse.
- The Reversal of Entropy: The "Prophet" that the people see (Verse 14) is actually the Invader. He halts the funeral procession—stopping the machinery of the Demiurge—and forces the gears of nature backward into Life.
- Unmerited Grace vs. Covenant Law: The motivation for this cosmic disruption is simple *"compassion"* (Verse 11). Jesus requires no statement of faith from the widow, no repentance from the dead man, and no sin offering. The Alien God is moved purely by the suffering inherent in the material world, acting entirely outside the boundaries of covenant obligation.

CHAPTER VII

The Rejection of John the Baptist

1 And the disciples of John shewed him of all these things.

2 And John calling unto him two of his disciples sent them to Jesus, saying, "Art thou he that should come? or look we for another?"

3 When the men were come unto him, they said, "John Baptist hath sent us unto thee, saying, 'Art thou he that should come? or look we for another?'"

4 And in that same hour he cured many of their infirmities and plagues, and of evil spirits; and unto many that were blind he gave sight.

5 Then Jesus answering said unto them, "Go your way, and tell John what things ye have seen and heard; how that the blind see, the lame walk, the lepers are cleansed, the deaf hear, the dead are raised, to the poor the gospel is preached."

6 "And blessed is he, whosoever shall not be offended in me."

7 And when the messengers of John were departed, he began to speak unto the people concerning John, "What went ye out into the wilderness for to see? A reed shaken with the wind?"

8 "But what went ye out for to see? A man clothed in soft raiment? Behold, they which are gorgeously apparelled, and live delicately, are in kings' courts."

9 "But what went ye out for to see? A prophet? Yea, I say unto you, and much more than a prophet."

10 "This is he, of whom it is written, 'Behold, I send my messenger before thy face, which shall prepare thy way before thee.'"

11 "For I say unto you, Among those that are born of women there is not a greater prophet than John the Baptist: but he that is least in the kingdom of God is greater than he."

The Sinful Woman & The Two Debtors

12 And one of the Pharisees desired him that he would eat with him. And he went into the Pharisee's house, and sat down to meat.

13 And, behold, a woman in the city, which was a sinner, when she knew that Jesus sat at meat in the Pharisee's house, brought an alabaster box of ointment,

14 And stood at his feet behind him weeping, and began to wash his feet with tears, and did wipe them with the hairs of her head, and kissed his feet, and anointed them with the ointment.

15 Now when the Pharisee which had bidden him saw it, he spake within himself, saying, "This man, if he were a prophet, would have known who and what manner of woman this is that toucheth him: for she is a sinner."

16 And Jesus answering said unto him, "Simon, I have somewhat to say unto thee." And he saith, "Master, say on."

17 "There was a certain creditor which had two debtors: the one owed five hundred pence, and the other fifty."

18 "And when they had nothing to pay, he frankly forgave them both. Tell me therefore, which of them will love him most?"

19 Simon answered and said, "I suppose that he, to whom he forgave most." And he said unto him, "Thou hast rightly judged."

20 And he turned to the woman, and said unto Simon, "Seest thou this woman? I entered into thine house, thou gavest me no water for my feet: but she hath washed my feet with tears, and wiped them with the hairs of her head."

21 "Thou gavest me no kiss: but this woman since the time I came in hath not ceased to kiss my feet."

22 "My head with oil thou didst not anoint: but this woman hath anointed my feet with ointment."

23 "Wherefore I say unto thee, Her sins, which are many, are forgiven; for she loved much: but to whom little is forgiven, the same loveth little."

24 And he said unto her, "Thy sins are forgiven."

25 And they that sat at meat with him began to say within themselves, "Who is this that forgiveth sins also?"

26 And he said to the woman, "Thy faith hath saved thee; go in peace."

Chapter VII Notes

The Demotion of John the Baptist (Verses 1–11) This sequence establishes the theological quarantine between the Old Testament and the Gospel, directly dismantling what the Prolegomenon identifies as the "Anchor of Prophecy."

- The Stranger: John the Baptist does not recognize Jesus. This is not a lapse in faith; it is a theological necessity. John is the "greatest born of women" (the highest product of the Creator's biological system), yet he is utterly blind to the spiritual reality of the Alien God. He is looking for the Demiurge's warrior; he finds the Father's healer.
- "Offended in Me" (Verse 6): The Greek *skandalisthe* implies a trap or stumbling block. John is "offended" because Jesus is not the Retributive Messiah promised by the Creator. He brings healing instead of judgment, confusing the prophet who was expecting the "axe laid to the root of the tree." The Prophetic Anchor fails to hold the Alien Christ.

The Great Separation (Verse 11) *"He that is least in the kingdom of God is greater than he."*

- The Two Dispensations: This verse is the definitive cut. John represents the absolute perfection of the Law and the zenith of the flesh. Yet, the lowliest pneumatic believer in the Alien God's Kingdom is spiritually superior to him. It proves that the Old and New Testaments are not a continuous slope, but two irreconcilable realities.

The Sinful Woman: Grace vs. Law (Verses 12–26) This narrative is the supreme demonstration of Grace actively superseding and invading the space of the Law.

- Simon the Pharisee: Represents the Creator's system—judgment based on statutes. He correctly identifies the woman as a "sinner" according to the Code, and he correctly notes that a "Prophet" of the Creator would shun her to maintain ritual purity.

- The Violation: Jesus fails Simon's test of a "Prophet" but reveals Himself as a "Savior." By allowing the woman to touch Him, He violates the Levitical laws of purity. He demonstrates that the Holiness of the Alien God is contagious (it cleanses the sinner on contact), whereas the Holiness of the Creator is defensive (it must avoid the sinner to survive).

The Two Debtors (Verses 17–18)

- The Mechanism of Salvation: In the Creator's system, debt must be strictly paid ("Eye for an Eye," or Temple blood sacrifice). In the Alien system, the Creditor "frankly forgives" (*echarisato*) both debtors when they have nothing to pay. Jesus usurps the Creator's economy by canceling the debt entirely without demanding a blood payment.
- "Thy Faith Hath Saved Thee" (Verse 26): In the Marcionite context, "Faith" (*pistis*) is the unique key to the New Kingdom. The Law condemns the woman; only Faith saves her.

Textual Restoration: The Exclusion of "Wisdom's Children"

- The Missing Text: The canonical comparison of "children in the marketplace" and the phrase "Wisdom is justified of all her children" (Luke 7:29–35) is excluded.
- Rationale: This orthodox interpolation attempts to link Jesus and John as two sides of the same coin ("Wisdom") to harmonize the two religions. Marcion rejected this linkage. Jesus and John played different tunes entirely—one a funeral dirge of the Law, the other a wedding dance of the Gospel—and they do not belong to the same God.

CHAPTER VIII

The Parable of the Sower

1 And it came to pass afterward, that he went throughout every city and village, preaching and shewing the glad tidings of the kingdom of God: and the twelve were with him,

2 And certain women, which had been healed of evil spirits and infirmities, Mary called Magdalene, out of whom went seven devils,

3 And Joanna the wife of Chuza Herod's steward, and Susanna, and many others, which ministered unto him of their substance.

4 And when much people were gathered together, and were come to him out of every city, he spake by a parable:

5 "A sower went out to sow his seed: and as he sowed, some fell by the way side; and it was trodden down, and the fowls of the air devoured it."

6 "And some fell upon a rock; and as soon as it was sprung up, it withered away, because it lacked moisture."

7 "And some fell among thorns; and the thorns sprang up with it, and choked it."

8 "And other fell on good ground, and sprang up, and bare fruit an hundredfold." And when he had said these things, he cried, "He that hath ears to hear, let him hear."

9 And his disciples asked him, saying, "What might this parable be?"

10 And he said, "Unto you it is given to know the mysteries of the kingdom of God: but to others in parables; that seeing they might not see, and hearing they might not understand."

11 "Now the parable is this: The seed is the word of God."

12 "Those by the way side are they that hear; then cometh the devil, and taketh away the word out of their hearts, lest they should believe and be saved."

13 "They on the rock are they, which, when they hear, receive the word with joy; and these have no root, which for a while believe, and in time of temptation fall away."

14 "And that which fell among thorns are they, which, when they have heard, go forth, and are choked with cares and riches and pleasures of this life, and bring no fruit to perfection."

15 "But that on the good ground are they, which in an honest and good heart, having heard the word, keep it, and bring forth fruit with patience."

The True Family of Christ

16 "No man, when he hath lighted a candle, covereth it with a vessel, or putteth it under a bed; but setteth it on a candlestick, that they which enter in may see the light."

17 "For nothing is secret, that shall not be made manifest; neither any thing hid, that shall not be known and come abroad."

18 Then came to him his mother and his brethren, and could not come at him for the press.

19 And it was told him by certain which said, "Thy mother and thy brethren stand without, desiring to see thee."

20 And he answered and said unto them, "Who is my mother and who are my brethren?"

21 And pointing to those around him, he said: "My mother and my brethren are these which hear the word of God, and do it."

Master of the Elements & The Legion

22 Now it came to pass on a certain day, that he went into a ship with his disciples: and he said unto them, "Let us go over unto the other side of the lake." And they launched forth.

23 But as they sailed he fell asleep: and there came down a storm of wind on the lake; and they were filled with water, and were in jeopardy.

24 And they came to him, and awoke him, saying, "Master, master, we perish." Then he arose, and rebuked the wind and the raging of the water: and they ceased, and there was a calm.

25 And he said unto them, "Where is your faith?" And they being afraid wondered, saying one to another, "What manner of man is this! for he commandeth even the winds and water, and they obey him."

26 And they arrived at the country of the Gadarenes, which is over against Galilee.

27 And when he went forth to land, there met him out of the city a
certain man, which had devils long time, and ware no clothes,
neither abode in any house, but in the tombs.

28 When he saw Jesus, he cried out, and fell down before him, and
with a loud voice said, "What have I to do with thee, Jesus, thou
Son of God most high? I beseech thee, torment me not."

29 (For he had commanded the unclean spirit to come out of the
man.)

30 And Jesus asked him, saying, "What is thy name?" And he said,
"Legion": because many devils were entered into him.

31 And they besought him that he would not command them to go
out into the deep.

32 And there was there an herd of many swine feeding on the
mountain: and they besought him that he would suffer them to
enter into them. And he suffered them.

33 Then went the devils out of the man, and entered into the swine:
and the herd ran violently down a steep place into the lake, and were
choked.

34 Then the whole multitude of the country of the Gadarenes
round about besought him to depart from them; for they were taken
with great fear: and he went up into the ship, and returned back
again.

The Woman with the Issue of Blood & Jairus' Daughter

35 And it came to pass, that, when Jesus was returned, the people gladly received him: for they were all waiting for him.

36 And, behold, there came a man named Jairus, and he was a ruler of the synagogue: and he fell down at Jesus' feet, and besought him that he would come into his house:

37 For he had one only daughter, about twelve years of age, and she lay a dying. But as he went the people thronged him.

38 And a woman having an issue of blood twelve years, which had spent all her living upon physicians, neither could be healed of any,

39 Came behind him, and touched the border of his garment: and immediately her issue of blood stanched.

40 And Jesus said, "Who touched me?" When all denied, Peter and they that were with him said, "Master, the multitude throng thee and press thee, and sayest thou, Who touched me?"

41 And Jesus said, "Somebody hath touched me: for I perceive that virtue is gone out of me."

42 And when the woman saw that she was not hid, she came trembling, and falling down before him, she declared unto him before all the people for what cause she had touched him, and how she was healed immediately.

43 And he said unto her, "Daughter, be of good comfort: thy faith hath made thee whole; go in peace."

44 While he yet spake, there cometh one from the ruler of the synagogue's house, saying to him, "Thy daughter is dead; trouble not the Master."

45 But when Jesus heard it, he answered him, saying, "Fear not: believe only, and she shall be made whole."

46 And when he came into the house, he suffered no man to go in, save Peter, and James, and John, and the father and the mother of the maiden.

47 And all wept, and bewailed her: but he said, "Weep not; she is not dead, but sleepeth."

48 And they laughed him to scorn, knowing that she was dead.

49 And he put them all out, and took her by the hand, and called, saying, "Maid, arise."

50 And her spirit came again, and she arose straightway: and he commanded to give her meat.

51 And her parents were astonished: but he charged them that they should tell no man what was done.

Chapter VIII Notes

The Parable of the Sower: The Hostile Terrain (Verses 5–15) This parable is the supreme illustration of the Alien Word entering the Creator's domain.

- The Alien Seed: The "Seed" is the Word of the Unknown God. It does not naturally belong to the soil of this world.
- The Demiurge's Defenses: The "Wayside," the "Rock," and the "Thorns" represent the hostile material mechanisms of the Creator's world—cares, riches, pleasures, and the Archon's agents (the "fowls of the air"/devils) designed to choke out the pneumatic Spirit.
- The Harvest: The "Good Ground" represents those rare souls who possess the *gnosis* to receive the Alien Word and produce fruit for a Kingdom outside this universe.

The Rejection of the Mother: Severing the Anchor of Flesh (Verses 19–21) *"Who is my mother and who are my brethren?"* This passage is the definitive Marcionite proof-text against the Incarnation, directly destroying what the Prolegomenon identifies as the Anchor of Flesh.

- The Trap: His "mother and brethren" arrive. In the orthodox context, this scene is used to establish His biological humanity (the Jamesian trap).
- The Refusal: Jesus's question *"Who is my mother?"* is not a rhetorical flourish; it is a literal theological deposition. He has no mother. He was not born of Mary. He descended from heaven fully formed (as established in Chapter I).
- The Redefinition: By pointing to those who "hear the word" as His true family, Jesus replaces the biological covenant (Israel/Lineage) with the spiritual covenant (Faith/Gnosis). The "True Family" is pneumatic, not genetic. The bonds of the Creator's flesh are nullified.

Master of the Elements (Verse 25) *"He commandeth even the winds and* water, *and they obey him."*

- The Supremacy: Jesus calms the storm not by praying to a "Father Creator" for help, but by issuing a direct command (*epitimao*—a rebuke).
- The Hostile Physics: This demonstrates that the Alien Son has intrinsic authority *over* the Creator's elements. The wind and water are not His creations; they are the hostile physics of the Demiurge, which He subjugates by force. He is not subject to natural law; He is its conqueror.

The Legion and the "Most High" (Verse 28) *"Jesus, thou Son of God most high."*

- The Title: The demons address Jesus as *Son of God Most High* (*Tou Theou Tou Hypsistou*).
- The Cosmological Distinction: In Marcionite theology, the demons—being spirits—recognize the Alien God immediately, while humans (blinded by the Creator's flesh) struggle to see Him. They identify Him not as the Jewish Messiah (the enforcer of the local Archon), but as the Son of the *Highest*—an invading deity infinitely superior to the god of the local territory.

"Who Touched Me?": The Alien's Ignorance (Verses 45–46) *"Somebody hath touched me: for I perceive that virtue is gone out of me."*

- The Cosmological Blindspot: Marcionites highlighted Jesus's question *"Who touched me?"* as forensic proof that He was not the Creator. The Creator (who built the material world) monitors every atom and legal infraction. The Alien God, being a Stranger to material causality, senses the extraction of His Spirit (*dynamis*) but does not monitor the physical crowd.
- Salvation by Theft: The woman is not healed by a formal Temple decree or a Levitical covenant; she "steals" the healing through raw Faith. The Alien God honors this unauthorized withdrawal of power because Faith—not Law—is the only currency He recognizes.

CHAPTER IX

The Mission of the Twelve

1 Then he called his twelve disciples together, and gave them power and authority over all devils, and to cure diseases.

2 And he sent them to preach the kingdom of God, and to heal the sick.

3 And he said unto them, "Take nothing for your journey, neither staves, nor scrip, neither bread, neither money; neither have two coats apiece."

4 "And whatsoever house ye enter into, there abide, and thence depart."

5 "And whosoever will not receive you, when ye go out of that city, shake off the very dust from your feet for a testimony against them."

6 And they departed, and went through the towns, preaching the gospel, and healing every where.

7 Now Herod the tetrarch heard of all that was done by him: and he was perplexed, because that it was said of some, that John was risen from the dead;

8 And of some, that Elias had appeared; and of others, that one of the old prophets was risen again.

9 And Herod said, "John have I beheaded: but who is this, of whom I hear such things?" And he desired to see him.

The Feeding of the Five Thousand

10 And the apostles, when they were returned, told him all that they had done. And he took them, and went aside privately into a desert place belonging to the city called Bethsaida.

11 And the people, when they knew it, followed him: and he received them, and spake unto them of the kingdom of God, and healed them that had need of healing.

12 And when the day began to wear away, then came the twelve, and said unto him, "Send the multitude away, that they may go into the towns and country round about, and lodge, and get victuals: for we are here in a desert place."

13 But he said unto them, "Give ye them to eat." And they said, "We have no more but five loaves and two fishes; except we should go and buy meat for all this people."

14 For they were about five thousand men. And he said to his disciples, "Make them sit down by fifties in a company."

15 And they did so, and made them all sit down.

16 Then he took the five loaves and the two fishes, and looking up to heaven, he blessed them, and brake, and gave to the disciples to set before the multitude.

17 And they did eat, and were all filled: and there was taken up of fragments that remained to them twelve baskets.

The Confession and The Transfiguration

18 And it came to pass, as he was alone praying, his disciples were with him: and he asked them, saying, "Whom say the people that I am?"

19 They answering said, "John the Baptist; but some say, Elias; and others say, that one of the old prophets is risen again."

20 He said unto them, "But whom say ye that I am?" Peter answering said, "The Christ of God."

21 And he straitly charged them, and commanded them to tell no man that thing;

22 Saying, "The Son of man must suffer many things, and be rejected of the elders and chief priests and scribes, and be slain, and be raised the third day."

23 And it came to pass about an eight days after these sayings, he took Peter and John and James, and went up into a mountain to pray.

24 And as he prayed, the fashion of his countenance was altered, and his raiment was white and glistering.

25 And, behold, there talked with him two men, which were Moses and Elias:

26 Who appeared in glory, and spake of his decease which he should accomplish at Jerusalem.

27 But Peter and they that were with him were heavy with sleep: and when they were awake, they saw his glory, and the two men that stood with him.

28 And it came to pass, as they departed from him, Peter said unto Jesus, "Master, it is good for us to be here: and let us make three tabernacles; one for thee, and one for Moses, and one for Elias": not knowing what he said.

29 While he thus spake, there came a cloud, and overshadowed them: and they feared as they entered into the cloud.

30 And there came a voice out of the cloud, saying, "This is my beloved Son: hear him."

31 And when the voice was past, Jesus was found alone. And they kept it close, and told no man in those days any of those things which they had seen.

The Failure of the Disciples

32 And it came to pass, that on the next day, when they were come down from the hill, much people met him.

33 And, behold, a man of the company cried out, saying, "Master, I beseech thee, look upon my son: for he is mine only child."

34 "And, lo, a spirit taketh him, and he suddenly crieth out; and it teareth him that he foameth again, and bruising him hardly departeth from him."

35 "And I besought thy disciples to cast him out; and they could not."

36 And Jesus answering said, "O faithless and perverse generation, how long shall I be with you, and suffer you? Bring thy son hither."

37 And as he was yet a coming, the devil threw him down, and tare him. And Jesus rebuked the unclean spirit, and healed the child, and delivered him again to his father.

38 And they were all amazed at the mighty power of God. But while they wondered every one at all things which Jesus did, he said unto his disciples,

39 "Let these sayings sink down into your ears: for the Son of man shall be delivered into the hands of men."

40 But they understood not this saying, and it was hid from them, that they perceived it not: and they feared to ask him of that saying.

The Rebuke of the Spirit of Elijah

41 And it came to pass, when the time was come that he should be received up, he steadfastly set his face to go to Jerusalem,

42 And sent messengers before his face: and they went, and entered into a village of the Samaritans, to make ready for him.

43 And they did not receive him, because his face was as though he would go to Jerusalem.

44 And when his disciples James and John saw this, they said, "Lord, wilt thou that we command fire to come down from heaven, and consume them, even as Elias did?"

45 But he turned, and rebuked them, and said, "Ye know not what manner of spirit ye are of."

46 "For the Son of man is not come to destroy men's lives, but to save them."

47 And they went to another village.

48 And it came to pass, that, as they went in the way, a certain man said unto him, "Lord, I will follow thee whithersoever thou goest."

49 And Jesus said unto him, "Foxes have holes, and birds of the air have nests; but the Son of man hath not where to lay his head."

50 And he said unto another, "Follow me." But he said, "Lord, suffer me first to go and bury my father."

51 Jesus said unto him, "Let the dead bury their dead: but go thou and preach the kingdom of God."

52 And another also said, "Lord, I will follow thee; but let me first go bid them farewell, which are at home at my house."

53 And Jesus said unto him, "No man, having put his hand to the plough, and looking back, is fit for the kingdom of God.

Chapter IX Notes

The Feeding of the Multitude: The Alien Economy (Verses 12–17)

- The Creator's Economy: The Twelve advise Jesus to send the multitude away to *"buy meat"* in the villages. They are operating under the Demiurge's system of commerce, scarcity, and transactional exchange.
- The Spontaneous Grace: Jesus bypasses the marketplace entirely. He does not purchase food; He spontaneously generates it from almost nothing. This demonstrates that the Alien God is not bound by the material scarcity of the Creator's world. His economy is one of infinite, unmerited provision.

The Confession and the Silence (Verses 18–21)

- The Misunderstood Title: Peter declares Jesus is *"The Christ of God."* However, Peter is still utilizing the dictionary of the Creator. He expects the "Christ" to be the Davidic warrior who will crush Rome and restore Israel.
- The Gag Order: Jesus immediately *"straitly charged them, and commanded them to tell no man."* This is not modesty; it is a tactical blackout. Because the disciples fundamentally misunderstand the nature of His mission, any preaching they do will falsely advertise Him as the Creator's Messiah. The Alien God must remain incognito until the work of the Cross is finished.

The Transfiguration: Severing the Anchor of Prophecy (Verses 25–30) Ecclesiastical tradition interprets this scene as Moses and Elijah validating Jesus. The forensic reading reveals it as a formal decommissioning of the Old Testament.

- The Contrast of Glories: Moses (The Law) and Elijah (The Prophets) appear in the glory of the Creator, but they stand subordinate to the Alien Glory of the Son.
- Peter's Error: Peter attempts to build three tabernacles, effectively equalizing the Law, the Prophets, and the Gospel.

The text explicitly notes Peter *"knew not what he said"*—he failed to distinguish the New God from the old servants.

- The Command of Supersession: The Cloud overshadows (erases) the prophets, leaving Jesus standing absolutely alone. The Voice commands: *"Hear Him."* This is an exclusive, terminal imperative. The timeline of Jewish prophecy is severed. Do not hear Moses anymore. Do not hear Elijah anymore. Hear *only* the Son.

The Rejection of the "Pillars": The Spirit of Elijah (Verses 44–46) This sequence is the smoking gun of Marcionite dualism: the explicit, undeniable rejection of the Old Testament Spirit.

- The Culprits (James and John): It is no coincidence that James and John—the very men who would later become the legalistic "Pillars" of the Jerusalem Church that Paul fought (Galatians 2)—are the ones who demand violence. They represent the "Anchors of Flesh and Time".
- The Biblical Precedent: They ask to call down fire from heaven *"even as Elias did."* They are acting in perfect, orthodox accordance with the Creator's scripture (2 Kings 1).
- The Verdict: Jesus rebukes them, declaring: *"Ye know not what manner of spirit ye are of."* * The Two Gods Defined: The retained text—*"For the Son of man is not come to destroy men's lives, but to save them"*—defines the ontological chasm. The Spirit of the Creator (Elijah) is a spirit of retributive fire and destruction. The Spirit of the Alien God (Jesus) is one of salvation. They are two mutually exclusive Spirits serving two different Gods.

"Foxes Have Holes" (Verse 49) *"The Son of man hath not where to lay his head."*

- The Homeless God: The foxes and birds are creatures of the Demiurge; they have "holes" and "nests" because they are biologically and legally at home in the material creation.
- The Alien: The Son of Man has no home here. He owns no property, holds no territory, and finds no rest in the domain of the Creator. He is a pure Stranger in a hostile universe.

"Let the Dead Bury Their Dead": Severing the Anchor of Flesh (Verses 50–51)

- The Supreme Duty: The disciple asks to fulfill the highest moral and biological obligation of the Jewish Law: burying one's father (honoring the lineage of the flesh).
- The Refusal: Jesus strictly forbids it. By calling the man's physical relatives *"the dead,"* Jesus categorizes the entire biological cycle of the Creator—birth, reproduction, and death—as a sprawling graveyard.
- The Implication: Service to the Alien God supersedes the most sacred ties of blood and DNA. The believer is called to completely sever the "Anchor of Flesh" and abandon the system of mortality entirely.

"Looking Back" (Verse 53)

- The Plough: The Kingdom requires absolute, forward-facing detachment. *"Looking back"* is to look toward the Creator's world, the security of the Law, and the biological family. To look back at the material world is to tether oneself to it, instantly disqualifying the soul from the spiritual Pleroma.

CHAPTER X

The Sending of the Seventy

1 After these things the Lord appointed other seventy also, and sent them two and two before his face into every city and place, whither he himself would come.

2 Therefore said he unto them, "The harvest truly is great, but the labourers are few: pray ye therefore the Lord of the harvest, that he would send forth labourers into his harvest."

3 "Go your ways: behold, I send you forth as lambs among wolves."

4 "Carry neither purse, nor scrip, nor shoes: and salute no man by the way."

5 "And into whatsoever house ye enter, first say, 'Peace be to this house.'"

6 "And if the son of peace be there, your peace shall rest upon it: if not, it shall turn to you again."

7 "And in the same house remain, eating and drinking such things as they give: for the labourer is worthy of his hire. Go not from house to house."

8 "And into whatsoever city ye enter, and they receive you, eat such things as are set before you:"

9 "And heal the sick that are therein, and say unto them, 'The kingdom of God is come nigh unto you.'"

10 "But into whatsoever city ye enter, and they receive you not, go your ways out into the streets of the same, and say,"

11 "'Even the very dust of your city, which cleaveth on us, we do wipe off against you: notwithstanding be ye sure of this, that the kingdom of God is come nigh unto you.'"

12 "But I say unto you, that it shall be more tolerable in that day for Sodom, than for that city."

16 "He that heareth you heareth me; and he that despiseth you despiseth me; and he that despiseth me despiseth him that sent me."

17 And the seventy returned again with joy, saying, "Lord, even the devils are subject unto us through thy name."

18 And he said unto them, "I beheld Satan as lightning fall from heaven."

19 "Behold, I give unto you power to tread on serpents and scorpions, and over all the power of the enemy: and nothing shall by any means hurt you."

20 "Notwithstanding in this rejoice not, that the spirits are subject unto you; but rather rejoice, because your names are written in heaven."

The Revelation of the Father

21 In that hour Jesus rejoiced in spirit, and said, "I thank thee, O Father, Lord of heaven and earth, that thou hast hid these things from the wise and prudent, and hast revealed them unto babes: even so, Father; for so it seemed good in thy sight."

22 And he turned him unto his disciples, and said privately, "All things are delivered to me of my Father: and no man knoweth who the Son is, but the Father; and who the Father is, but the Son, and he to whom the Son will reveal him."

The Lawyer and the Good Samaritan

25 And, behold, a certain lawyer stood up, and tempted him, saying, "Master, what shall I do to inherit eternal life?"

26 He said unto him, "What is written in the law? how readest thou?"

27 And he answering said, "Thou shalt love the Lord thy God with all thy heart, and with all thy soul, and with all thy strength, and with all thy mind; and thy neighbour as thyself."

28 And he said unto him, "Thou hast answered right: this do, and thou shalt live."

29 But he, willing to justify himself, said unto Jesus, "And who is my neighbour?"

30 And Jesus answering said, "A certain man went down from Jerusalem to Jericho, and fell among thieves, which stripped him of his raiment, and wounded him, and departed, leaving him half dead."

31 "And by chance there came down a certain priest that way: and when he saw him, he passed by on the other side."

32 "And likewise a Levite, when he was at the place, came and looked on him, and passed by on the other side."

33 "But a certain Samaritan, as he journeyed, came where he was: and when he saw him, he had compassion on him,"

34 "And went to him, and bound up his wounds, pouring in oil and wine, and set him on his own beast, and brought him to an inn, and took care of him."

35 "And on the morrow when he departed, he took out two pence, and gave them to the host, and said unto him, 'Take care of him; and whatsoever thou spendest more, when I come again, I will repay thee.'"

36 "Which now of these three, thinkest thou, was neighbour unto him that fell among the thieves?"

37 And he said, "He that shewed mercy on him." Then said Jesus unto him, "Go, and do thou likewise."

Chapter X Notes

The Seventy: The Pauline Vanguard (Verse 1) The appointment of the Seventy is a deliberate, hostile act of supersession against the religious establishment.

- The Symbolism: The Twelve Apostles correspond to the Twelve Tribes of Israel (the Creator's specific, localized domain). The number Seventy corresponds to the traditional Jewish count of the "Nations of the World" (Gentiles).
- The Replacement of the Pillars: By empowering the Seventy, Jesus signals that the containment field of Israel has failed. The Twelve—who are tethered to the Anchor of Flesh (James) and the Law—fail to understand the Spirit. The Seventy represent the Authentic Voice of Paul: a cosmic, boundary-breaking mission to the Gentiles that bypasses the authority of Jerusalem entirely.

"Satan as Lightning": The Breaking of the Grid (Verse 18) *"I beheld Satan as* lightning *fall from heaven."*

- The Invasion: This is the cosmological pivot of the *Evangelion*. Until this moment, the Creator/Satan ruled the lower heavens (the material universe) unchallenged.
- The Event: The success of the Seventy—who wielded the power of the Alien Name against the "devils" of this world—marks the real-time breaking of the Archon's power. Jesus is not predicting a distant, future eschatological event; He is observing the immediate, tactical collapse of the Creator's defense grid as the Alien Spirit invades.

The Revelation of the Unknown God: Severing the Anchor of Prophecy (Verses 21–22) This passage is the theological bedrock of the Marcionite reconstruction. It completely vaporizes the orthodox claim that Jesus was the fulfillment of the Old Testament.

- The Hidden Truth: Jesus thanks the Father for hiding the truth from the *"wise and prudent"* (the scribes, Pharisees, and prophets of the Creator) and revealing it to *"babes"* (the pneumatics, untainted by the Law).
- "No Man Knoweth": This is the definitive statement of the *Deus Absconditus* (The Hidden God).
- The Forensic Proof: If the Father of Jesus were the Creator of the Old Testament, He would be intimately known by every Jewish priest and prophet. The fact that *no one* knows the Father proves He is a completely different, previously unrevealed Deity. He is the Stranger. Consequently, the Old Testament prophets could not possibly have prophesied about Him. The Anchor of Prophecy is severed.

"Lord of Heaven" (Verse 21)

- The Variant: The canonical text reads *"Father, Lord of heaven and earth."* A strict Marcionite reading likely excised *"and earth."*
- The Reason: The Alien Father is the Lord of the Pleroma (Heaven/Spirit), but He is explicitly *not* the architect of the material Earth (Matter). To call Him "Lord of Earth" would falsely equate Him with the Demiurge.

The Good Samaritan: The Indictment of the Law (Verses 30–37) This parable is retained not as a quaint moral lesson, but as a stinging, forensic attack on the Levitical system itself.

- The Crime Scene (Jerusalem to Jericho): The road descends from Jerusalem (the seat of the Creator's Temple). The Priest and the Levite are traveling *from* the epicenter of the Law.
- The Legal Trap: These men do not pass the bleeding man because they are unusually cruel; they pass him because they are *strictly observant*. According to the Creator's Law (Numbers 19:11), touching a corpse makes a man ritually unclean for seven days, disqualifying him from Temple service and separating him from the community. They are forced by the Creator to choose Ritual Purity (Law) over Compassion (Spirit). The Law literally mandates their apathy.

- The Heretic: The Samaritan is an outsider, a heretic to the Jewish Covenant (much like Marcion and Paul). He stops because he operates entirely outside the Creator's jurisdiction, motivated purely by Compassion—the primary attribute of the Alien God.
- The Conclusion: The Law of the Creator *prevents* love; the Spirit of the Alien God *mandates* it.

Purging the Lukan Spackle

- The Woes (Luke 10:13–15): The woes to Chorazin and Bethsaida are excised. These verses invoke Old Testament judgments (Tyre and Sidon) and portray Jesus as a condemning, retributive judge. This is an orthodox graft designed to make Jesus sound like a prophet of the Creator.
- Mary and Martha (Luke 10:38–42): This domestic scene is excised. It anchors Jesus in a biological, familial setting (the Anchor of Flesh), lacks cosmological utility, and interrupts the sharp transition from the radical ethics of the Samaritan directly to the spiritual instruction on Prayer in Chapter XI.

CHAPTER XI

The Prayer to the Father

1 And it came to pass, that, as he was praying in a certain place, when he ceased, one of his disciples said unto him, "Lord, teach us to pray, as John also taught his disciples."

2 And he said unto them, "When ye pray, say: Father, let thy Holy Spirit come upon us and cleanse us. Thy kingdom come. Thy will be done, as in heaven, so in earth."

3 "Give us day by day our daily bread."

4 "And forgive us our sins; for we also forgive every one that is indebted to us. And lead us not into temptation."

Asking and Receiving

5 And he said unto them, "Which of you shall have a friend, and shall go unto him at midnight, and say unto him, 'Friend, lend me three loaves;'"

6 "'For a friend of mine in his journey is come to me, and I have nothing to set before him?'"

7 "And he from within shall answer and say, 'Trouble me not: the door is now shut, and my children are with me in bed; I cannot rise and give thee.'"

8 "I say unto you, Though he will not rise and give him, because he is his friend, yet because of his importunity he will rise and give him as many as he needeth."

9 "And I say unto you, Ask, and it shall be given you; seek, and ye shall find; knock, and it shall be opened unto you."

10 "For every one that asketh receiveth; and he that seeketh findeth; and to him that knocketh it shall be opened."

11 "If a son shall ask bread of any of you that is a father, will he give him a stone? or if he ask a fish, will he for a fish give him a serpent?"

12 "Or if he shall ask an egg, will he offer him a scorpion?"

13 "If ye then, being evil, know how to give good gifts unto your children: how much more shall your Father give the Holy Spirit to them that ask him?"

The Beelzebub Controversy & The Strong Man

14 And he was casting out a devil, and it was dumb. And it came to pass, when the devil was gone out, the dumb spake; and the people wondered.

15 But some of them said, "He casteth out devils through Beelzebub the chief of the devils."

16 And others, tempting him, sought of him a sign from heaven.

17 But he, knowing their thoughts, said unto them, "Every kingdom divided against itself is brought to desolation; and a house divided against a house falleth."

18 "If Satan also be divided against himself, how shall his kingdom stand? because ye say that I cast out devils through Beelzebub."

19 "And if I by Beelzebub cast out devils, by whom do your sons cast them out? therefore shall they be your judges."

20 "But if I with the finger of God cast out devils, no doubt the kingdom of God is come upon you."

21 "When a strong man armed keepeth his palace, his goods are in peace:"

22 "But when a stronger than he shall come upon him, and overcome him, he taketh from him all his armour wherein he trusted, and divideth his spoils."

23 "He that is not with me is against me: and he that gathereth not with me scattereth."

The Rejection of Biological Blessedness

24 And it came to pass, as he spake these things, a certain woman of the company lifted up her voice, and said unto him, "Blessed is the womb that bare thee, and the paps which thou hast sucked."

25 But he said, "Yea rather, blessed are they that hear the word of God, and keep it."

The Refusal of a Sign (The Jonah Excision)

26 And when the people were gathered thick together, he began to say, "This is an evil generation: they seek a sign; and there shall no sign be given it."

The Light of the Body

27 "No man, when he hath lighted a candle, putteth it in a secret place, neither under a bushel, but on a candlestick, that they which come in may see the light."

28 "The light of the body is the eye: therefore when thine eye is single, thy whole body also is full of light; but when thine eye is evil, thy body also is full of darkness."

29 "Take heed therefore that the light which is in thee be not darkness."

The Woe to the Pharisees and Lawyers

30 And as he spake, a certain Pharisee besought him to dine with him: and he went in, and sat down to meat.

31 And when the Pharisee saw it, he marvelled that he had not first washed before dinner.

32 And the Lord said unto him, "Now do ye Pharisees make clean the outside of the cup and the platter; but your inward part is full of ravening and wickedness."

33 "Woe unto you, Pharisees! for ye tithe mint and rue and all manner of herbs, and pass over judgment and the love of God: these ought ye to have done, and not to leave the other undone."

34 "Woe unto you, Pharisees! for ye love the uppermost seats in the synagogues, and greetings in the markets."

35 "Woe unto you, scribes and Pharisees, hypocrites! for ye are as graves which appear not, and the men that walk over them are not aware of them."

36 Then answered one of the lawyers, and said unto him, "Master, thus saying thou reproachest us also."

37 And he said, "Woe unto you also, ye lawyers! for ye lade men with burdens grievous to be borne, and ye yourselves touch not the burdens with one of your fingers."

38 "Woe unto you! for ye build the sepulchres of the prophets, and your fathers killed them."

39 "Truly ye bear witness that ye allow the deeds of your fathers: for they indeed killed them, and ye build their sepulchres."

40 "Woe unto you, lawyers! for ye have taken away the key of knowledge: ye entered not in yourselves, and them that were entering in ye hindered."

Chapter XI Notes

The Marcionite Lord's Prayer: The Usurpation of Worship (Verse 2) The orthodox version of this prayer (Matthew 6) is a petition to the Creator. The *Evangelion* version is a plea for spiritual transmutation.

- The Omission of the Name: The address to the Creator as the provider (*"Hallowed be thy name"*) is excised. Marcion associated the obsession with the "Name" with the Jewish God's jealousy and demand for legalistic reverence.
- The Substitution: The text substitutes *"Let thy Holy Spirit come upon us and cleanse us."* This changes the prayer from an act of bureaucratic submission toward a distant Archon into a plea for immediate pneumatic liberation.

"If Ye Then, Being Evil" (Verse 13)

- The Nature of Humanity: Marcion seized upon this verse to demonstrate that the nature of the Creator's material world is fundamentally flawed. Jesus casually calls His own audience *"evil"* (*poneroi*). He does not mean they are uniquely bad individuals; He means their very biological/material nature is corrupt.
- The Cosmic Contrast: If "evil" biological fathers—operating within the Demiurge's broken system—can still care for their children, how much more will the "Good" Father (who is entirely outside this world) provide the Spirit? This establishes the ontological superiority of the Alien God over the natural order.

The Allegory of the Strong Man: The Cosmic Raid (Verses 21–22)

This parable is the central cosmological claim of the *Evangelion*. It explicitly defines the mission of the Alien Christ not as a peaceful reform, but as a violent home invasion.

- The Strong Man: Represents the Creator (the Demiurge), who rules this material world (his *"palace"*) and keeps human souls (*"his goods"*) under the lock and key of the Law and the Flesh.
- The Raid: The *"Stronger One"* is the Alien God (Jesus). He does not negotiate with the Creator, nor does He pay a ransom to him. He invades.
- The Spoils: Salvation is depicted forensically as a robbery. Jesus defeats the Creator, strips him of his *"armor"* (the authority of the Prophets and the Law), and *"divides the spoils"*—stealing humanity away from its original, legal master.

"Blessed is the Womb": Severing the Anchor of Flesh (Verses 27–28)

- The Trap: A woman in the crowd attempts to praise Jesus's physical origin (*"Blessed is the womb that bare thee"*). This is the exact theological trap identified in the Prolegomenon: the Anchor of Flesh, the attempt to bind the Alien Christ to biology and a human mother.
- The Rejection: Jesus immediately and forcefully rejects the "blessing of the womb." He counters: *"Yea rather, blessed are they that hear the word of God, and keep it."*
- The Forensic Reality: In the Old Testament, biological fertility and lineage were the highest signs of the Creator's favor. In the New Kingdom, biology is completely worthless. Jesus publicly cuts the biological tether to Mary, proving He is pure Ideology descending from above, unrelated to human reproduction.

The Refusal of the Sign: Severing the Anchor of Prophecy (Verse 29)

- The Orthodox Spackle: In Canonical Luke and Matthew, Jesus compares Himself to the prophet Jonah (*"For as Jonas was a sign unto the Ninevites..."*). This is a classic orthodox interpolation designed to stitch Jesus into the Jewish prophetic timeline (the Anchor of Prophecy).

- The Marcionite Excision: Applying *Lectio Brevior Potior*, the original, uncorrupted text reveals a hard stop: *"They seek a sign; and there shall no sign be given it."* * The Rationale: The Alien God does not rely on the "types and shadows" of the Old Testament to validate His mission. He refuses to be historicized. He offers no prophetic proof to an "evil generation" other than the sheer, unmediated presence of the Light itself.

The Key of Knowledge (Verse 52) *"Ye have taken away the key of knowledge."*

- The Indictment: Marcion interpreted the "Key" as the *gnosis* (realization) that the Creator is not the Supreme God.
- The Wardens: The lawyers and scribes (experts in the Law) suppressed this truth. By enforcing strict adherence to the Torah, they locked the people inside the Creator's system (the prison mentioned in your preface) and actively prevented them from entering the higher Kingdom of the Alien Father.

CHAPTER XII

The Leaven of the Pharisees & The True Fear

1 In the mean time, when there were gathered together an innumerable multitude of people, insomuch that they trode one upon another, he began to say unto his disciples first of all, "Beware ye of the leaven of the Pharisees, which is hypocrisy."

2 "For there is nothing covered, that shall not be revealed; neither hid, that shall not be known."

3 "Therefore whatsoever ye have spoken in darkness shall be heard in the light; and that which ye have spoken in the ear in closets shall be proclaimed upon the housetops."

4 "And I say unto you my friends, Be not afraid of them that kill the body, and after that have no more that they can do."

5 "But I will forewarn you whom ye shall fear: Fear him, which after he hath killed hath power to cast into hell; yea, I say unto you, Fear him."

6 "Are not five sparrows sold for two farthings, and not one of them is forgotten before God?"

7 "But even the very hairs of your head are all numbered. Fear not therefore: ye are of more value than many sparrows."

8 "Also I say unto you, Whosoever shall confess me before men, him shall the Son of man also confess before the angels of God:"

9 "But he that denieth me before men shall be denied before the angels of God."

10 "And whosoever shall speak a word against the Son of man, it shall be forgiven him: but unto him that blasphemeth against the Holy Ghost it shall not be forgiven."

11 "And when they bring you unto the synagogues, and unto magistrates, and powers, take ye no thought how or what thing ye shall answer, or what ye shall say:"

12 "For the Holy Ghost shall teach you in the same hour what ye ought to say."

The Refusal to Judge & The Rich Fool

13 And one of the company said unto him, "Master, speak to my brother, that he divide the inheritance with me."

14 And he said unto him, "Man, who made me a judge or a divider over you?"

15 And he said unto them, "Take heed, and beware of covetousness: for a man's life consisteth not in the abundance of the things which he possesseth."

16 And he spake a parable unto them, saying, "The ground of a certain rich man brought forth plentifully:"

17 "And he thought within himself, saying, 'What shall I do, because I have no room where to bestow my fruits?'"

18 "And he said, 'This will I do: I will pull down my barns, and build greater; and there will I bestow all my fruits and my goods.'"

19 "And I will say to my soul, 'Soul, thou hast much goods laid up for many years; take thine ease, eat, drink, and be merry.'"

20 "But God said unto him, 'Thou fool, this night thy soul shall be required of thee: then whose shall those things be, which thou hast provided?'"

21 "So is he that layeth up treasure for himself, and is not rich toward God."

Care for the Soul vs. The Cares of the World

22 And he said unto his disciples, "Therefore I say unto you, Take no thought for your life, what ye shall eat; neither for the body, what ye shall put on."

23 "The life is more than meat, and the body is more than raiment."

24 "Consider the ravens: for they neither sow nor reap; which neither have storehouse nor barn; and God feedeth them: how much more are ye better than the fowls?"

25 "And which of you with taking thought can add to his stature one cubit?"

26 "If ye then be not able to do that thing which is least, why take ye thought for the rest?"

27 "Consider the lilies how they grow: they toil not, they spin not; and yet I say unto you, that Solomon in all his glory was not arrayed like one of these."

28 "If then God so clothe the grass, which is to day in the field, and to morrow is cast into the oven; how much more will he clothe you, O ye of little faith?"

29 "And seek not ye what ye shall eat, or what ye shall drink, neither be ye of doubtful mind."

30 "For all these things do the nations of the world seek after: and your Father knoweth that ye have need of these things."

31 "But rather seek ye the kingdom of God; and all these things shall be added unto you."

32 "Fear not, little flock; for it is your Father's good pleasure to give you the kingdom."

33 "Sell that ye have, and give alms; provide yourselves bags which wax not old, a treasure in the heavens that faileth not, where no thief approacheth, neither moth corrupteth."

34 "For where your treasure is, there will your heart be also."

The Watchful Servants

35 "Let your loins be girded about, and your lights burning;"

36 "And ye yourselves like unto men that wait for their lord, when he will return from the wedding; that when he cometh and knocketh, they may open unto him immediately."

37 "Blessed are those servants, whom the lord when he cometh shall find watching: verily I say unto you, that he shall gird himself, and make them to sit down to meat, and will come forth and serve them."

38 "And if he shall come in the second watch, or come in the third watch, and find them so, blessed are those servants."

39 "And this know, that if the goodman of the house had known
what hour the thief would come, he would have watched, and not
have suffered his house to be broken through."

40 "Be ye therefore ready also: for the Son of man cometh at an
hour when ye think not."

The Fire and the Division

49 "I am come to send fire on the earth; and what will I, if it be
already kindled?"

50 "But I have a baptism to be baptized with; and how am I
straitened till it be accomplished!"

51 "Suppose ye that I am come to give peace on earth? I tell you,
Nay; but rather division:"

52 "For from henceforth there shall be five in one house divided,
three against two, and two against three."

53 "The father shall be divided against the son, and the son against
the father; the mother against the daughter, and the daughter
against the mother; the mother in law against her daughter in law,
and the daughter in law against her mother in law."

Discerning the Time

54 And he said also to the people, "When ye see a cloud rise out of
the west, straightway ye say, 'There cometh a shower'; and so it is."

55 "And when ye see the south wind blow, ye say, 'There will be heat'; and it came to pass."

56 "Ye hypocrites, ye can discern the face of the sky and of the earth; but how is it that ye do not discern this time?"

57 "Yea, and why even of yourselves judge ye not what is right?"

Chapter XII Notes

The Refusal to Judge: Jurisdictional Denial (Verse 14) *"Man, who made me a judge or a divider over you?"*

- The Orthodox Problem: In the Old Testament, the Creator God is the ultimate Judge and Divider of lands (e.g., Joshua's division of Canaan, the laws of inheritance in Numbers 27).
- The Theological Implication: When asked to settle a legal dispute about earthly inheritance, Jesus explicitly refuses the jurisdiction. The Alien God deals only with the Spirit; He flatly refuses to participate in the legal, economic, or material administration of the Creator's world. Earthly property is the Demiurge's concern.

"Fear Him": Intel on the Warden (Verse 5) *"Fear him, which after he hath killed hath power to cast into hell."*

- The Forensic Dualism: Orthodox theology assumes Jesus is warning people to fear *His* Father. Marcionites recognized this as an absurdity—the Good Father does not cast souls into fire. Marcion preserved this warning but interpreted the "Him" as the Creator (the Demiurge).
- The Warning: Jesus is providing tactical intel on the enemy. Do not fear the Roman magistrates or the Pharisees, who can only kill the biological body. Fear the Creator, the Warden of this universe, who possesses the legal authority of Gehenna. The Alien God's role is to *rescue* souls from this Warden, not to act as His executioner.

The Rich Fool: The Cosmic Creditor (Verse 20) *"But God said unto him... thy soul shall be required of thee."*

- The Transaction of Death: The speaker here is "God" (the Creator of the material world). The Greek term for "required" (*apaitousin*) is strict banking terminology; it implies a commercial loan being called in with interest.

- The Lesson: The Rich Fool prospered perfectly within the Creator's biological and economic system. Now, the Creator demands His capital (the biological life-force) back. The Alien God has no part in this transaction. It reveals the Creator's world as a temporary, fatal lease.

The Ravens and Lilies: The Anti-Economy (Verses 24–27) This passage creates a sharp cosmological contrast between the anxiety of the "nations of the world" and the "Little Flock."

- The Contrast of Systems: The "nations" serve the Creator and are subjected to His economy of scarcity, labor, and anxiety (the curse of Genesis 3: "By the sweat of your brow").
- The Argument A Fortiori: If the strict, transactional Creator feeds the ravens (unclean birds under the Law), how much more will the Good, Non-Transactional Father sustain those who possess His Spirit? The Alien God operates an economy of spontaneous grace, nullifying the Creator's economy of anxious labor.

The Fire and Division: Severing the Anchor of Flesh (Verses 49–53) This violent imagery is the practical application of the Great Severance, directly attacking what the Anchor of Flesh.

- The Disruption of Biology: The "Peace" of the Creator's world is based entirely on the biological family, lineage, reproduction, and the passing down of the Law from father to son. Jesus declares He has come to send "Fire" on the earth to incinerate this system.
- Literal Division: *"The father shall be divided against the son..."* Jesus actively wields a sword against the biological family unit. For Marcionite Christians—whose strict asceticism and rejection of marriage often broke up traditional Jewish and Roman families—this was not a metaphor; it was a lived, necessary reality. To join the True Family (Spirit), one must abandon the Creator's Family (DNA).

"Paying the Last Mite": The Orthodox Spackle (Omitted Verses 58–59)

- The Exclusion: The canonical text includes a warning to "agree with thine adversary" to avoid the judge, the prison, and paying *"the last mite."* Following the principle of *Lectio Brevior Potior*, this is excised as a later Lukan/Orthodox addition.
- The Forensic Rationale: This passage explicitly validates the system of debt, courts, and retributive justice (*Lex Talionis*). The Alien God operates exclusively on Grace, freely canceling all debts (as seen in the Parable of the Two Debtors). To suggest that a soul must pay "the last mite" is to trap them right back in the Creator's legalism. Jesus came to break the prison, not to teach inmates how to pay their bail.

CHAPTER XIII

Repentance and The Barren Fig Tree

1 There were present at that season some that told him of the Galileans, whose blood Pilate had mingled with their sacrifices.

2 And Jesus answering said unto them, "Suppose ye that these Galileans were sinners above all the Galileans, because they suffered such things?"

3 "I tell you, Nay: but, except ye repent, ye shall all likewise perish."

4 "Or those eighteen, upon whom the tower in Siloam fell, and slew them, think ye that they were sinners above all men that dwelt in Jerusalem?"

5 "I tell you, Nay: but, except ye repent, ye shall all likewise perish."

6 He spake also this parable; "A certain man had a fig tree planted in his vineyard; and he came and sought fruit thereon, and found none."

7 "Then said he unto the dresser of his vineyard, 'Behold, these three years I come seeking fruit on this fig tree, and find none: cut it down; why cumbereth it the ground?'"

8 "And he answering said unto him, 'Lord, let it alone this year also, till I shall dig about it, and dung it:'"

9 "'And if it bear fruit, well: and if not, then after that thou shalt cut it down.'"

The Woman Bowed by Satan

10 And he was teaching in one of the synagogues on the sabbath.

11 And, behold, there was a woman which had a spirit of infirmity eighteen years, and was bowed together, and could in no wise lift up herself.

12 And when Jesus saw her, he called her to him, and said unto her, "Woman, thou art loosed from thine infirmity."

13 And he laid his hands on her: and immediately she was made straight, and glorified God.

14 And the ruler of the synagogue answered with indignation, because that Jesus had healed on the sabbath day, and said unto the people, "There are six days in which men ought to work: in them therefore come and be healed, and not on the sabbath day."

15 The Lord then answered him, and said, "Thou hypocrite, doth not each one of you on the sabbath loose his ox or his ass from the stall, and lead him away to watering?"

16 "And ought not this woman, being a daughter of Abraham, whom Satan hath bound, lo, these eighteen years, be loosed from this bond on the sabbath day?"

17 And when he had said these things, all his adversaries were ashamed: and all the people rejoiced for all the glorious things that were done by him.

The Mustard Seed and The Leaven

18 Then said he, "Unto what is the kingdom of God like? and whereunto shall I resemble it?"

19 "It is like a grain of mustard seed, which a man took, and cast into his garden; and it grew, and waxed a great tree; and the fowls of the air lodged in the branches of it."

20 And again he said, "Whereunto shall I liken the kingdom of God?"

21 "It is like leaven, which a woman took and hid in three measures of meal, till the whole was leavened."

The Narrow Door and The Exclusion

22 And he went through the cities and villages, teaching, and journeying toward Jerusalem.

23 Then said one unto him, "Lord, are there few that be saved?" And he said unto them,

24 "Strive to enter in at the strait gate: for many, I say unto you, will seek to enter in, and shall not be able."

25 "When once the master of the house is risen up, and hath shut to the door, and ye begin to stand without, and to knock at the door, saying, 'Lord, Lord, open unto us'; and he shall answer and say unto you, 'I know you not whence ye are':"

26 "Then shall ye begin to say, 'We have eaten and drunk in thy presence, and thou hast taught in our streets.'"

27 "But he shall say, 'I tell you, I know you not whence ye are; depart from me, all ye workers of iniquity.'"

28 "There shall be weeping and gnashing of teeth, when ye shall see all the just in the kingdom of God, and you yourselves thrust out."

29 "And they shall come from the east, and from the west, and from the north, and from the south, and shall sit down in the kingdom of God."

30 "And, behold, there are last which shall be first, and there are first which shall be last."

The Lament over Jerusalem

31 The same day there came certain of the Pharisees, saying unto him, "Get thee out, and depart hence: for Herod will kill thee."

32 And he said unto them, "Go ye, and tell that fox, 'Behold, I cast out devils, and I do cures to day and to morrow, and the third day I shall be perfected.'"

33 "Nevertheless I must walk to day, and to morrow, and the day following: for it cannot be that a prophet perish out of Jerusalem."

34 "O Jerusalem, Jerusalem, which killest the prophets, and stonest them that are sent unto thee; I would I have gathered thy children together, as a hen doth gather her brood under her wings, and ye would not!"

35 "Behold, your house is left unto you desolate: and verily I say unto you, Ye shall not see me, until the time come when ye shall say, 'Blessed is he that cometh in the name of the Lord.'"

Chapter XIII Notes

The Barren Fig Tree: The Great Severance (Verses 6–9)

- The Allegory of Failure: The "Certain Man" (the Owner) represents the Creator. The "Fig Tree" represents Israel, planted in the center of the Creator's vineyard.
- The Verdict: The Creator has sought righteousness (fruit) from His chosen people for centuries through the Law, but found only empty ritual. The Demiurge's socio-religious experiment has failed.
- The Sentence: The command to *"Cut it down; why cumbereth it the ground?"* is the narrative justification for the Great Severance. The Old Covenant is not being pruned or fertilized by the Alien Son; it is being earmarked for total destruction because its dead roots strangle the soil where the New Faith must grow.

The "Daughter of Abraham": Severing the Anchor of Flesh (Verse 16) "Ought *not this woman, being a daughter of Abraham, whom Satan hath bound..."*

- The Biological Diagnosis: Jesus explicitly links her physical ailment with her physical lineage. To be a "Daughter of Abraham" is to be anchored to the Covenant of the Flesh. The DNA of the Patriarchs is synonymous with the bondage of the Archon (Satan).
- The Loosing: Jesus *"looses"* her not just from a spinal curvature, but from the crushing weight of her ancestry. He shatters the Sabbath (the Creator's sacred time) to physically free her from Abraham (the Creator's biological chain). It is a double-assault on the orthodox anchors.

The Exclusion of the Patriarchs (Verse 28)

- The Orthodox Spackle: The canonical text includes the names *"Abraham, Isaac, and Jacob"* sitting in the Kingdom. According to the principle of *Lectio Brevior Potior*, this is a blatant orthodox interpolation designed to seamlessly stitch the New Kingdom to the Old Testament founders.
- The Restoration: The Marcionite text surgically removes the Patriarchs.
- The Cosmological Rationale: The Jewish Patriarchs were faithful servants of the Demiurge. They knew nothing of the Alien Father. Therefore, they remain in the Creator's underworld (Hades) and are denied entry into the Pleroma.
- The Shock of the New: The *"weeping and gnashing of teeth"* occurs because the religious establishment expects to see their founders in the seats of honor. Instead, they find them entirely absent, while "Strangers" (Gentiles) from the four winds occupy the Kingdom. The lineage is voided.

The Lament over Jerusalem: Severing the Anchor of Time (Verse 34)

- The Interpolation of "How Often": The canonical text reads, *"How often would I have gathered thy children together..."* This phrase is excised as a later historicizing graft.
- The Forensic Reason: Paul explicitly taught that the Christ was a *"mystery kept secret since the world began"* (Romans 16:25). The Alien God had zero prior interaction with Israel. To have Jesus claim He tried "often" to gather them in the past (via the prophets) would mutate Him into the Creator-God of the Old Testament. It re-establishes the Anchor of Prophecy.
- The Reconstruction: Stripped of the Lukan spackle, the lament is restored to its proper, immediate scope: Jesus offered the Kingdom to Jerusalem during His *present* invasion, but they rejected the Stranger just as they traditionally killed the Creator's own prophets.

"Your House is Left Desolate": The Final Divorce (Verse 35)

- The Abandonment: Jesus refers to the Temple specifically as *"Your house,"* completely distancing the Alien Father from it. It is no longer the "House of God"; it is merely a stone building belonging to the Jews.
- The Desolation: By declaring it *"desolate,"* Jesus formally announces the withdrawal of all divine presence. The Spirit evacuates the premises. The subsequent historical destruction of Jerusalem by the Romans is merely the physical collapse of a structure that had already been spiritually condemned by the Alien God.

CHAPTER XIV

Sabbath Healing

1 And it came to pass, as he went into the house of one of the chief Pharisees to eat bread on the sabbath day, that they watched him.

2 And, behold, there was a certain man before him which had the dropsy.

3 And Jesus answering spake unto the lawyers and Pharisees, saying, "Is it lawful to heal on the sabbath day?"

4 And they held their peace. And he took him, and healed him, and let him go;

5 And answered them, saying, "Which of you shall have an ass or an ox fallen into a pit, and will not straightway pull him out on the sabbath day?"

6 And they could not answer him again to these things.

Parable of Choosing Places

7 And he put forth a parable to those which were bidden, when he marked how they chose out the chief rooms; saying unto them,

8 "When thou art bidden of any man to a wedding, sit not down in the highest room; lest a more honourable man than thou be bidden of him;"

9 "And he that bade thee and him come and say to thee, 'Give this man place'; and thou begin with shame to take the lowest room."

10 "But when thou art bidden, go and sit down in the lowest room; that when he that bade thee cometh, he may say unto thee, 'Friend, go up higher': then shalt thou have worship in the presence of them that sit at meat with thee."

11 "For whosoever exalteth himself shall be abased; and he that humbleth himself shall be exalted."

Parable of the Dinner

12 Then said he also to him that bade him, "When thou makest a dinner or a supper, call not thy friends, nor thy brethren, neither thy kinsmen, nor thy rich neighbours; lest they also bid thee again, and a recompence be made thee."

13 "But when thou makest a feast, call the poor, the maimed, the lame, the blind:"

14 "And thou shalt be blessed; for they cannot recompense thee: for thou shalt be recompensed at the resurrection of the just."

15 And when one of them that sat at meat with him heard these things, he said unto him, "Blessed is he that shall eat bread in the kingdom of God."

16 Then said he unto him, "A certain man made a great supper, and bade many:"

17 "And sent his servant at supper time to say to them that were bidden, 'Come; for all things are now ready.'"

18 "And they all with one consent began to make excuse. The first said unto him, 'I have bought a piece of ground, and I must needs go and see it: I pray thee have me excused.'"

19 "And another said, 'I have bought five yoke of oxen, and I go to prove them: I pray thee have me excused.'"

20 "And another said, 'I have married a wife, and therefore I cannot come.'"

21 "So that servant came, and shewed his lord these things. Then the master of the house being angry said to his servant, 'Go out quickly into the streets and lanes of the city, and bring in hither the poor, and the maimed, and the halt, and the blind.'"

22 "And the servant said, 'Lord, it is done as thou hast commanded, and yet there is room.'"

23 "And the lord said unto the servant, 'Go out into the highways and hedges, and compel them to come in, that my house may be filled.'"

24 "For I say unto you, That none of those men which were bidden shall taste of my supper."

Sayings on Discipleship

25 And there went great multitudes with him: and he turned, and said unto them,

26 "If any man come to me, and hate not his father, and mother, and wife, and children, and brethren, and sisters, yea, and his own life also, he cannot be my disciple."

27 "And whosoever doth not bear his cross, and come after me, cannot be my disciple."

33 "So likewise, whosoever he be of you that forsaketh not all that he hath, he cannot be my disciple."

Chapters XIV Notes

Sabbath Healing: The Hypocrisy of Property (Verses 1–6)

- The Panopticon: *"They watched him"* (Verse 1). Jesus is under surveillance by the Wardens of the Law (the Pharisees). They are waiting for Him to commit a ritual crime.
- The Economic Checkmate: Jesus preempts their accusation by asking if they would pull a fallen ass or ox out of a pit on the Sabbath.
- The Indictment of the Law: Jesus exposes a fatal moral flaw in the Creator's Law: The Law makes exemptions for the preservation of *property* and *livestock*, but it strictly forbids the relief of *human suffering* (the man with the dropsy). Jesus demonstrates that the Creator's system values economic assets over pneumatic souls. He heals the man, completely dismissing the sanctity of the Creator's calendar.

The Parable of the Dinner: The Trinity of Traps (Verses 16–24) The excuses made by the invited guests (the establishment) constitute a total rejection of the Spirit in favor of the Creator's material institutions.

- The Trinity of Traps:
    1. Land: *"I have bought a piece of ground."* (Attachment to Territory/Nationalism).
    2. Labor: *"I have bought five yoke of oxen."* (Attachment to Economy/Commerce).
    3. Flesh: *"I have married a wife."* (Attachment to Biology/Reproduction).
- The Fatal Excuse: Note that the man who marries a wife (Verse 20) does not even ask to be excused; he flatly states, *"I cannot come."* Marcion argued that biological reproduction is the strongest chain the Demiurge possesses. Marriage is not merely a distraction; it is a hard disqualification from the Pleroma because it actively participates in the Creator's trap of pulling more souls into the prison of the flesh.

- "Compel Them to Come In" (Verse 23): The Master commands the servant to *"compel"* (*anagkason*) the poor and maimed to enter. This is not religious coercion; it is an emergency rescue. The "House" of the Alien God is the only lifeboat in a universe earmarked for destruction. The servant must aggressively drag the broken souls out of the Creator's "highways and hedges" before the system collapses.

Severing the Anchor of Flesh: "Hating" the Family (Verse 26) *"If any man come to me, and hate not his father, and mother, and wife, and children... he cannot be my disciple."*

- The Strict Reading: The text retains the literal *"hate"* (*misei*), fiercely rejecting the orthodox attempt to soften the translation to "love less."
- The Destruction of the Jamesian Trap: This is the explicit theological destruction of the Anchor of Flesh. The biological family is the primary structure of the Creator's world. Parents are the biological agents who trapped the pneumatic Spirit in flesh.
- The Spiritual Necessity: To embrace the Alien Father, one must violently sever the emotional, legal, and genetic ties that bind the soul to the Demiurge's cycle of generation. This is not emotional malice; it is the prerequisite for spiritual liberation. You cannot be a citizen of the Spirit while holding a passport of the Flesh.

Total Liquidation: The Cross and the Assets (Verses 27, 33) *"Whosoever he be of you that forsaketh not all that he hath, he cannot be my disciple."*

- The Instrument of Execution (Verse 27): To "bear his cross" is not a metaphor for enduring daily inconveniences. The Cross was the Roman instrument for executing rebels. Jesus demands that His followers consider themselves legally dead to the Empire and the Creator's world.
- The Liquidation of Assets (Verse 33): Forsaking all that one has is not an act of charity to improve the world; it is the total liquidation of assets in a bankrupt universe. You cannot hold currency in the Creator's economy and simultaneously follow the Alien God.

CHAPTER XV

The Lost Sheep & The Lost Coin

1 Then drew near unto him all the publicans and sinners for to hear him.

2 And the Pharisees and scribes murmured, saying, "This man receiveth sinners, and eateth with them."

3 And he spake this parable unto them, saying,

4 "What man of you, having an hundred sheep, if he lose one of them, doth not leave the ninety and nine in the wilderness, and go after that which is lost, until he find it?"

5 "And when he hath found it, he layeth it on his shoulders, rejoicing."

6 "And when he cometh home, he calleth together his friends and neighbours, saying unto them, 'Rejoice with me; for I have found my sheep which was lost.'"

7 "I say unto you, that likewise joy shall be in heaven over one sinner that repenteth, more than over ninety and nine just persons, which need no repentance."

8 "Either what woman having ten pieces of silver, if she lose one piece, doth not light a candle, and sweep the house, and seek diligently till she find it?"

9 "And when she hath found it, she calleth her friends and her neighbours together, saying, 'Rejoice with me; for I have found the piece which I had lost.'"

10 "Likewise, I say unto you, there is joy in the presence of the angels of God over one sinner that repenteth."

Chapter XV Notes

The Omission of the Prodigal Son: Rejecting the Harmonization Trap (Luke 15:11–32)

- The Missing Text: The famous "Parable of the Prodigal Son" is strictly excluded from this reconstruction. Following the principle of *Lectio Brevior Potior*, it is identified as a massive, later orthodox interpolation.
- The Orthodox Agenda: The canonical parable was designed by the proto-orthodox church to harmonize the two covenants. The "Elder Brother" represents Israel (The Law), and the "Younger Brother" represents the Gentiles (The Church). By placing them both in the same house, under the same Father, the Lukan editor attempts to definitively crush the Marcionite thesis of the Two Gods.
- The Forensic Rationale: The Alien God has zero historical relationship with Israel. He could not validly say to the Elder Brother (the Pharisees/Lawyers), *"Son, thou art ever with me, and all that I have is thine."* He was a total Stranger to them until the fifteenth year of Tiberius. To leave this parable in the text is to surrender to the Creator.

The Lost Sheep: The Abandonment of the "Just" (Verses 4–7)

- The Definition of the "Just": The *"ninety and nine just persons"* (*dikaios*) are those who successfully and strictly follow the Law of the Creator (the Pharisees). They "need no repentance" because, within the closed system of the Creator's retributive Justice, they are already sufficient. They have kept the rules of the biological and legal prison.
- The Abandonment: Notice the geography: The Shepherd leaves the ninety and nine *"in the wilderness"* (the desolate domain of the Creator, echoing Sinai). He does not come to reform or patch the flock of the Law; He actively abandons them to go steal the one "Lost" soul away from it.

- The Cosmic Scandal: The Alien God intentionally bypasses the righteous, law-abiding majority. The "Joy in Heaven" is not for the maintenance of the Demiurge's religious order, but for the retrieval of a pneumatic soul that was never truly meant for the Creator's fold.

The Lost Coin: Sweeping the Demiurge's House (Verses 8–10)

- The Allegory of Matter: The "House" represents the darkened, material universe of the Creator. The "Piece of Silver" (drachma) is the pneumatic spark—the spirit—that has fallen and become trapped in the dirt of the biological world.
- The Invasion of Light: The "Candle" is the sudden, illuminating intrusion of the Alien Gospel into the Creator's dark domain.
- The Agitation: The Woman *"sweeps the house"* to find the silver. This implies disruption. The value of the soul is hidden under the accumulated filth of the Demiurge's laws, anxieties, and flesh. It requires the invasive, agitating Light of the Stranger to uncover it and pull it out of the dirt.

CHAPTER XVI

The Unjust Steward

1 And he said also unto his disciples, "There was a certain rich man, which had a steward; and the same was accused unto him that he had wasted his goods."

2 And he called him, and said unto him, "How is it that I hear this of thee? give an account of thy stewardship; for thou mayest be no longer steward."

3 Then the steward said within himself, "What shall I do? for my lord taketh away from me the stewardship: I cannot dig; to beg I am ashamed."

4 "I am resolved what to do, that, when I am put out of the stewardship, they may receive me into their houses."

5 So he called every one of his lord's debtors unto him, and said unto the first, "How much owest thou unto my lord?"

6 And he said, "An hundred measures of oil." And he said unto him, "Take thy bill, and sit down quickly, and write fifty."

7 Then said he to another, "And how much owest thou?" And he said, "An hundred measures of wheat." And he said unto him, "Take thy bill, and write fourscore."

8 And the lord commended the unjust steward, because he had done wisely: for the children of this world are in their generation wiser than the children of light.

9 "And I say unto you, Make to yourselves friends of the mammon of unrighteousness; that, when ye fail, they may receive you into everlasting habitations."

10 "He that is faithful in that which is least is faithful also in much: and he that is unjust in the least is unjust also in much."

11 "If therefore ye have not been faithful in the unrighteous mammon, who will commit to your trust the true riches?"

12 "And if ye have not been faithful in that which is another man's, who shall give you that which is your own?"

13 "No servant can serve two masters: for either he will hate the one, and love the other; or else he will hold to the one, and despise the other. Ye cannot serve God and mammon."

The End of the Law

16 "The law and the prophets were until John: since that time the kingdom of God is preached, and every man presseth into it."

The Rich Man and Lazarus

19 "There was a certain rich man, which was clothed in purple and fine linen, and fared sumptuously every day:"

20 "And there was a certain beggar named Lazarus, which was laid at his gate, full of sores,"

21 "And desiring to be fed with the crumbs which fell from the rich man's table: moreover the dogs came and looked upon his sores."

22 "And it came to pass, that the beggar died, and was carried by the angels. The rich man also died, and was buried;"

23 "And in hell he lift up his eyes, being in torments, and seeth a certain poor man."

24 "And he cried and said, 'Father, have mercy on me, and send Lazarus, that he may dip the tip of his finger in water, and cool my tongue; for I am tormented in this flame.'"

25 "But it was said to him, 'Child, remember that thou in thy lifetime receivedst thy good things, and likewise Lazarus evil things: but now he is comforted, and thou art tormented.'"

26 "'And beside all this, between us and you there is a great gulf fixed: so that they which would pass from hence to you cannot; neither can they pass to us, that would come from thence.'"

28 "'For I have five brethren; that he may testify unto them, lest they also come into this place of torment.'"

29 "He said unto him, 'They have Moses and the prophets; let them hear them.'"

30 "And he said, 'Nay, father: but if one went unto them from the dead, they will repent.'"

31 "And he said unto him, 'If they hear not Moses and the prophets, neither will they be persuaded, though one rose from the dead.'"

Chapter XVI Notes

The Unjust Steward: Hacking the Creator's Economy (Verses 1–9) Orthodox commentators have spent two millennia trying to explain why Jesus praises a corrupt accountant. In the Marcionite forensic reading, this parable is a masterpiece of cosmic subversion and a survival manual for the pneumatic soul.

- The Cast: The "Rich Man" is the Creator (the Demiurge), the ruthless landlord of the material world. The "Steward" is the enlightened believer (the Gnostic) who realizes his time in the physical body is expiring.
- The Debt Strike: The Creator demands strict, 100% payment of the Law (100 measures of oil/wheat). The Believer knows this legalistic debt is impossible to pay and leads only to the prison of Hades. The "Unjust" act—fraudulently reducing the debtors' ledgers to 50 or 80—represents the preaching of Alien Grace.
- The Cosmic Heist: By canceling the debts owed to the Creator, the Believer secures a future outside the system. Jesus commands His followers to use "Unrighteous Mammon" (the material currency of the Demiurge) to cheat the Creator of His strict legal dues. You cannot win by playing by the Creator's rules; you must hack the ledger with unmerited mercy.

"That Which is Another Man's" (Verse 12) *"And if ye have not been* faithful *in that which is another man's, who shall give you that which is your own?"*

- The Alien World: The text explicitly refers to the entire material world, including the biological body, as *"that which is another man's."* * The Anthropological Truth: This confirms the absolute dualism of Paul and Marcion: we are strangers trapped in a foreign jurisdiction. The physical world legally belongs to the Creator; only the invisible Spirit is *"our own."* The Great Severance: Terminating the Anchor of Prophecy (Verse 16) *"The law and the prophets were until John: since that time the kingdom of God is preached..."*

- The Expiration Date: This surviving verse is the linchpin of the Marcionite timeline. It establishes that the administration of the Creator (the Law and the Prophets) had a hard, definitive expiration date: the ministry of John the Baptist.
- The Total Discontinuity: *"Since that time,"* an entirely new, alien frequency is being broadcast. The two eras do not overlap, merge, or evolve. The Kingdom of the Alien God completely replaces the Dominion of the Law. The Old Testament is not fulfilled; its jurisdiction is permanently terminated.

The Great Omission: Purging the Orthodox Spackle (Verses 14–18)

- The Orthodox Contradiction (The Law): The canonical text contains a glaringly un-Pauline block of sayings insisting that *"it is easier for heaven and earth to pass, than one tittle of the law to fail."* Following *Lectio Brevior Potior*, this is the clumsiest orthodox interpolation in the text. The Alien God did not descend to immortalize the Creator's prison. To claim the Law is eternal is to trap the Spirit in matter forever.
- The Divorce Sayings (The Flesh): The canonical rules regulating divorce are equally excised. Why? Because they presuppose the authority and sanctity of the Creator's biological institutions (marriage and reproduction). The New Kingdom does not regulate the flesh; it transcends it entirely.

The Rich Man and Lazarus: The Bankruptcy of the Law (Verses 19–31) This is not a parable about wealth; it is a live demonstration of the failure of the Creator's salvation mechanism.

- The Excision of "Abraham's Bosom" (Verse 22): The canonical phrase is surgically removed. Abraham was a patriarch of the Creator; he plays no role in the salvation of the Alien God. Lazarus is carried simply "by angels" to a place of spiritual respite, completely severed from the Jewish lineage.
- The Removal of the Patriarch (Verses 24-31): The canonical text features the Rich Man speaking to "Father Abraham." The original text features the Rich Man speaking simply to *"Father"*—the Creator Himself, the architect of this underworld.

- The Limit of the System: The dialogue exposes the fatal limitation of the Creator's system. When asked to send a rescue mission to the living, the Creator can only offer His legal code: *"They have Moses and the prophets; let them hear them."* The Rich Man knows this is useless (*"Nay, father"*), but the Demiurge has nothing else to give. He has no Grace, only the Scroll.
- The Final Indictment: *"If they hear not Moses and the prophets, neither will they be persuaded, though one rose from the dead."* This is the ultimate condemnation of the orthodox mindset. Those whose ears are tuned strictly to the frequency of the Creator (Moses) are biologically incapable of hearing the Alien frequency of the Resurrection.

CHAPTER XVII

Offenses and Forgiveness

1 Then said he unto the disciples, "It is impossible but that offences will come: but woe unto him, through whom they come!"

2 "It were better for him that a millstone were hanged about his neck, and he cast into the sea, than that he should offend one of these little ones."

3 "Take heed to yourselves: If thy brother trespass against thee, rebuke him; and if he repent, forgive him."

4 "And if he trespass against thee seven times in a day, and seven times in a day turn again to thee, saying, 'I repent'; thou shalt forgive him."

The Power of Faith

5 And the apostles said unto the Lord, "Increase our faith."

6 And the Lord said, "If ye had faith as a grain of mustard seed, ye might say unto this sycamine tree, 'Be thou plucked up by the root, and be thou planted in the sea'; and it should obey you."

7 "But which of you, having a servant plowing or feeding cattle, will say unto him by and by, when he is come from the field, 'Go and sit down to meat?'"

8 "And will not rather say unto him, 'Make ready wherewith I may sup, and gird thyself, and serve me, till I have eaten and drunken; and afterward thou shalt eat and drink?'"

9 "Doth he thank that servant because he did the things that were commanded him? I trow not."

10 "So likewise ye, when ye shall have done all those things which are commanded you, say, 'We are unprofitable servants: we have done that which was our duty to do.'"

The Ten Lepers (The Samaritan's Gratitude)

11 And it came to pass, as he went to Jerusalem, that he passed through the midst of Samaria and Galilee.

12 And as he entered into a certain village, there met him ten men that were lepers, which stood afar off:

13 And they lifted up their voices, and said, "Jesus, Master, have mercy on us."

14 And when he saw them, he said unto them, "Go shew yourselves unto the priests." And it came to pass, that, as they went, they were cleansed.

15 And one of them, when he saw that he was healed, turned back, and with a loud voice glorified God,

16 And fell down on his face at his feet, giving him thanks: and he was a Samaritan.

17 And Jesus answering said, "Were there not ten cleansed? but where are the nine?"

18 "There are not found that returned to give glory to God, save this stranger."

19 And he said unto him, "Arise, go thy way: thy faith hath made thee whole."

The Nature of the Kingdom

20 And when he was demanded of the Pharisees, when the kingdom of God should come, he answered them and said, "The kingdom of God cometh not with observation:"

21 "Neither shall they say, 'Lo here!' or, 'lo there!' for, behold, the kingdom of God is within you."

22 And he said unto the disciples, "The days will come, when ye shall desire to see one of the days of the Son of man, and ye shall not see it."

23 "And they shall say to you, 'See here'; or, 'see there': go not after them, nor follow them."

24 "For as the lightning, that lighteneth out of the one part under heaven, shineth unto the other part under heaven; so shall also the Son of man be in his day."

25 "But first must he suffer many things, and be rejected of this generation."

26 "And as it was in the days of Noe, so shall it be also in the days of the Son of man."

27 "They did eat, they drank, they married wives, they were given in marriage, until the day that Noe entered into the ark, and the flood came, and destroyed them all."

28 "Likewise also as it was in the days of Lot; they did eat, they drank, they bought, they sold, they planted, they builded;"

29 "But the same day that Lot went out of Sodom it rained fire and brimstone from heaven, and destroyed them all."

30 "Even thus shall it be in the day when the Son of man is revealed."

31 "In that day, he which shall be upon the housetop, and his stuff in the house, let him not come down to take it away: and he that is in the field, let him likewise not return back."

32 "Remember Lot's wife."

33 "Whosoever shall seek to save his life shall lose it; and whosoever shall lose his life shall preserve it."

34 "I tell you, in that night there shall be two men in one bed; the one shall be taken, and the other shall be left."

35 "Two women shall be grinding together; the one shall be taken, and the other left."

37 And they answered and said unto him, "Where, Lord?" And he said unto them, "Wheresoever the body is, thither will the eagles be gathered together."

Chapter XVII Notes

The Millstone: The Severity of the Spiritual Crime (Verses 1–2) *"It were better for him that a millstone were hanged about his neck..."*

- The Crime: To "offend" (*skandalisei*) one of the "little ones" does not mean to hurt their feelings; in the Marcionite context, it means to trap a pneumatic soul (a child of the Light) back into the legalism and flesh of the Creator's system.
- The Execution: The imagery of the heavy millstone cast into the sea represents total, inescapable submersion into the Abyss (the chaotic material realm of the Demiurge). It is a fate worse than physical death.

The Unprofitable Servant: The Bankruptcy of the Law (Verses 7–10) This parable is a devastating critique of the Creator's covenant and its transactional economy.

- The Slave Logic: The relationship between the Creator and His people is strictly one of Master and Slave. The servant works the field (the material world) and demands his wages.
- The Zero-Sum Game: Jesus points out that even if a Jew keeps every single letter of the Torah (*"doing all that was commanded"*), they have earned absolutely nothing extra. They are still merely an *"unprofitable servant"* who only did the bare minimum to avoid punishment.
- The Contrast: The Law can only produce obedient, terrified slaves. It has no mechanism to produce Sons. It requires the unmerited Grace of the Alien God to change a soul's ontology from Slave to Heir.

The Ten Lepers: The Trap of Levitical Obedience (Verses 11–19) This miracle perfectly encapsulates the failure of the Jewish Law and the triumph of the Stranger.

- The Nine (The Law): The nine Jewish lepers represent the "Righteous" under the Law. Jesus tells them to *"shew yourselves unto the priests,"* and they obey. They receive physical cleansing, but by strictly adhering to the Creator's ritual trajectory (Leviticus 14), they completely miss the Savior. Their obedience to the Law blinds them to Grace.
- The Stranger (The Spirit): The Samaritan represents the Gentile/Alien convert. He breaks the prescribed ritual trajectory. He realizes that the true Priest is not in the Temple in Jerusalem. He returns to Jesus.
- The Verdict: Jesus highlights that the "Stranger" alone recognized the True God. The blessing *"Thy faith hath made thee whole"* is reserved exclusively for the one who abandoned the Creator's Priests to worship the Alien Spirit.

"The Kingdom of God is Within You" (Verses 20–21) *"The kingdom of God cometh not with observation."*

- Anti-Geographic & Anti-Prophetic: The Pharisees demand to know *when* the Kingdom will arrive. The Creator's Kingdom is tied to land, temples, military victories, and chronological prophecy (*"Lo here! Lo there!"*). Jesus denies this entirely. The Alien God has no territory on this earth and operates on no Jewish timeline.
- The Interior Reality: The Greek *entos hymon* indicates the Kingdom is a spiritual spark residing *inside* the believer. It is not a future political event in Jerusalem; it is a present, internal, pneumatic reality accessed by cutting ties with the material world.

The Days of Noah and Lot: Severing the Anchor of Flesh (Verses 26–30) Jesus cites the Creator's own history to warn against the trap of the Creator's world.

- The Destroyer: It is the God of Genesis (the Demiurge) who sends Floods and Fire to judge His own biological property. The material world is a ticking time bomb of the Creator's wrath.

- The Distraction of Biology: The list of doomed activities—*"they did eat, they drank, they married wives, they were given in marriage"*—defines the exact trap of material existence. Notice that these are not "sins" under the Law; they are the standard biological imperatives of the Demiurge.
- Encratism (Asceticism): The specific condemnation of "marrying" reinforces the Marcionite view that biological reproduction (the Anchor of Flesh) is a fatal distraction that binds the soul to a world destined for destruction.

"Remember Lot's Wife" (Verse 32)

- The Backward Glance: Lot's wife was destroyed because she looked back at Sodom. She was emotionally and materially attached to the world she was supposed to be fleeing.
- The Absolute Command: The pneumatic believer must exit the Creator's world without a single shred of nostalgia. To "look back" at the life of the flesh, the biological family, or the Law, is to instantly perish with it. Total detachment is the only path to the Pleroma.

CHAPTER XVIII

The Parable of the Persistent Widow

1 And he spake a parable unto them to this end, that men ought always to pray, and not to faint;

2 Saying, "There was in a city a judge, which feared not God, neither regarded man:"

3 "And there was a widow in that city; and she came unto him, saying, 'Avenge me of mine adversary.'"

4 "And he would not for a while: but afterward he said within himself, 'Though I fear not God, nor regard man;'"

5 "'Yet because this widow troubleth me, I will avenge her, lest by her continual coming she weary me.'"

6 And the Lord said, "Hear what the unjust judge saith."

7 "And shall not God avenge his own elect, which cry day and night unto him, though he bear long with them?"

8 "I tell you that he will avenge them speedily. Nevertheless, when the Son of man cometh, shall he find faith on the earth?"

The Pharisee and the Publican

9 And he spake this parable unto certain which trusted in themselves that they were righteous, and despised others:

10 "Two men went up into the temple to pray; the one a Pharisee, and the other a publican."

11 "The Pharisee stood and prayed thus with himself, 'God, I thank thee, that I am not as other men are, extortioners, unjust, adulterers, or even as this publican.'"

12 "'I fast twice in the week, I give tithes of all that I possess.'"

13 "And the publican, standing afar off, would not lift up so much as his eyes unto heaven, but smote upon his breast, saying, 'God be merciful to me a sinner.'"

14 "I tell you, this man went down to his house justified rather than the other: for every one that exalteth himself shall be abased; and he that humbleth himself shall be exalted."

Jesus Blesses the Children

15 And they brought unto him also infants, that he would touch them: but when his disciples saw it, they rebuked them.

16 But Jesus called them unto him, and said, "Suffer little children to come unto me, and forbid them not: for of such is the kingdom of God."

17 "Verily I say unto you, Whosoever shall not receive the kingdom of God as a little child shall in no wise enter therein."

The Rich Ruler

18 And a certain ruler asked him, saying, "Good Master, what shall I do to inherit eternal life?"

19 And Jesus said unto him, "Why callest thou me good? None is good, save one, that is, God the Father."

20 "Thou knowest the commandments, Do not commit adultery, Do not kill, Do not steal, Do not bear false witness, Honor thy father and thy mother."

21 And he said, "All these have I kept from my youth up."

22 Now when Jesus heard these things, he said unto him, "Yet lackest thou one thing: sell all that thou hast, and distribute unto the poor, and thou shalt have treasure in heaven: and come, follow me."

23 And when he heard this, he was very sorrowful: for he was very rich.

24 And when Jesus saw that he was very sorrowful, he said, "How hardly shall they that have riches enter into the kingdom of God!"

25 "For it is easier for a camel to go through a needle's eye, than for a rich man to enter into the kingdom of God."

26 And they that heard it said, "Who then can be saved?"

27 And he said, "The things which are impossible with men are possible with God."

The Reward of Discipleship

28 Then Peter said, "Lo, we have left all, and followed thee."

29 And he said unto them, "Verily I say unto you, There is no man that hath left house, or parents, or brethren, or wife, or children, for the kingdom of God's sake,"

30 "Who shall not receive manifold more in this present time, and in the world to come life everlasting."

The Third Prediction of the Passion

31 Then he took unto him the twelve, and said unto them, "Behold, we go up to Jerusalem, and the Son of man shall be delivered unto the Gentiles, and shall be mocked, and spitefully entreated, and spitted on:"

32 "And they shall scourge him, and put him to death: and the third day he shall rise again."

33 And they understood none of these things: and this saying was hid from them, neither knew they the things which were spoken.

The Blind Man at Jericho

35 And it came to pass, that as he was come nigh unto Jericho, a certain blind man sat by the way side begging:

36 And hearing the multitude pass by, he asked what it meant.

37 And they told him, that Jesus of Nazareth passeth by.

38 And he cried, saying, "Jesus, thou Son of David, have mercy on me."

39 And they which went before rebuked him, that he should hold his peace: but he cried so much the more, "Thou Son of David, have mercy on me."

40 And Jesus stood, and commanded him to be brought unto him:
and when he was come near, he asked him,

41 Saying, "What wilt thou that I shall do unto thee?" And he said,
"Lord, that I may receive my sight."

42 And Jesus said unto him, "Receive thy sight: thy faith hath saved
thee."

43 And immediately he received his sight, and followed him,
glorifying God: and all the people, when they saw it, gave praise
unto God.

Chapter XVIII Notes

The Unjust Judge: The Character of the Demiurge (Verses 1–8) While orthodox tradition reads this as a lesson on persistence in prayer, Marcionites viewed this parable as a dark, accurate description of the Creator God's system.

- The Demiurge: The Judge represents the God of this world—a being who admits he *"feared not God, neither regarded man."* He rules strictly by Law and annoyance, not by Love.
- The Transaction of Weariness: The Creator demands constant petition, blood sacrifice, and legal groveling before He grants justice. He only acts lest the petitioner *"weary me."* * The Contrast: The parable sharply contrasts the reluctant, transactional nature of the Creator with the character of the Alien Father, who gives unmerited Grace freely and speedily to His elect.

The Pharisee and the Publican: The Bankruptcy of Righteousness (Verses 9–14)

This parable systematically dismantles the Creator's system of merit.

- The Pharisee (The Law): The Pharisee represents the absolute peak of Demiurgic religion. He is not lying; he has perfectly executed the Creator's Law (fasting, tithing, avoiding extortion). Yet, his perfection within the Creator's system produces only arrogance.
- The Publican (Grace): The tax collector is totally bankrupt in the Creator's economy. He has no legal merit. He does not offer a sacrifice; he simply begs for unmerited mercy.
- The Verdict: Jesus declares the bankrupt man "justified" over the perfect man. This proves that success in the Creator's religion is actually an impediment to the Alien God's Kingdom.

The Rich Ruler: The Ontological Chasm (Verses 18–27) *"Why callest thou me good? None is good, save one, that is, God the Father."*

- The Ultimate Proof-Text: This is the theological cornerstone of the *Evangelion*. When the Ruler calls Jesus "Good," Jesus immediately corrects him using the strict ontological definitions of Marcionite dualism.
- Just vs. Good: The Creator God of the Old Testament is "Just" (administering *Lex Talionis*, an eye for an eye). He is never "Good" (giving unmerited favor to the guilty). By stating *"None is good, save one,"* Jesus definitively separates the attribute of Goodness from the Creator, proving that His Father is a completely different, previously unknown entity.
- The Insufficiency of the Law: The Ruler has perfectly kept the Creator's civil commandments (*"All these have I kept"*). Yet, Jesus reveals he still lacks Eternal Life. The Law of Moses possesses no life-giving power; it merely regulates the flesh.
- Total Liquidation: Jesus demands he sell everything. The Creator's material currency (wealth) cannot be transferred into the Pleroma. It is easier to defy the laws of physics (a camel through a needle's eye) than to bring the Demiurge's assets into the Alien Kingdom.

Severing the Anchor of Flesh: The Reward of Discipleship (Verses 28–30)

- The Rejection of the Family: Peter points out that they have left everything. Jesus promises manifold rewards to anyone who has left *"house, or parents, or brethren, or wife, or children."*
- Encratism as Liberation: The believer must actively abandon the biological structures of the Creator—marriage, lineage, and reproduction—to be adopted into the Kingdom.

The Blindness of the Apostles (Verses 31–33) *"And they understood none of these things: and this saying was hid from them..."*

- The Prophetic Failure: Jesus plainly predicts His suffering and death. Yet the Twelve (the future pillars of the Orthodox church) are completely blind to it. Why?
- The Wrong Paradigm: Because they are tethered to the Anchor of Prophecy. They expect the Creator's Messiah to conquer Rome and establish a global Jewish empire. The concept of an Alien God submitting to the executioners of the Demiurge to purchase souls is completely outside their theological framework.

The Blind Man at Jericho: The "Son of David" Misunderstanding (Verses 35–43)

- The Double Blindness: The beggar is physically blind, but more importantly, he is theologically blind. He repeatedly identifies Jesus using the orthodox Anchor of Prophecy: *"Son of David."*
- The Unmerited Cure: Does Jesus correct the title here? No. Jesus heals him out of pure, unconditioned Mercy, despite the man using the incorrect, Demiurgic title. The scene perfectly illustrates that Israel, trapped in the dark, could only reach out to the Stranger by fumbling through the distorted, inadequate vocabulary of their own national prophecies.

CHAPTER XIX

Zacchaeus the Publican

1 And Jesus entered and passed through Jericho.

2 And, behold, there was a man named Zacchaeus, which was the chief among the publicans, and he was rich.

3 And he sought to see Jesus who he was; and could not for the press, because he was little of stature.

4 And he ran before, and climbed up into a sycamore tree to see him: for he was to pass that way.

5 And when Jesus came to the place, he looked up, and saw him, and said unto him, "Zacchaeus, make haste, and come down; for today I must abide at thy house."

6 And he made haste, and came down, and received him joyfully.

7 And when they saw it, they all murmured, saying, "That he was gone to be guest with a man that is a sinner."

8 And Zacchaeus stood, and said unto the Lord; "Behold, Lord, the half of my goods I give to the poor; and if I have taken any thing from any man by false accusation, I restore him fourfold."

9 And Jesus said unto him, "This day is salvation come to this house."

10 "For the Son of man is come to seek and to save that which was lost."

The Parable of the Pounds

11 And as they heard these things, he added and spake a parable, because he was nigh to Jerusalem, and because they thought that the kingdom of God should immediately appear.

12 He said therefore, "A certain nobleman went into a far country to receive for himself a kingdom, and to return."

13 "And he called his ten servants, and delivered them ten pounds, and said unto them, 'Occupy till I come.'"

14 "But his citizens hated him, and sent a message after him, saying, 'We will not have this man to reign over us.'"

15 "And it came to pass, that when he was returned, having received the kingdom, then he commanded these servants to be called unto him, to whom he had given the money, that he might know how much every man had gained by trading."

16 "Then came the first, saying, 'Lord, thy pound hath gained ten pounds.'"

17 "And he said unto him, 'Well, thou good servant: because thou hast been faithful in a very little, have thou authority over ten cities.'"

18 "And the second came, saying, 'Lord, thy pound hath gained five pounds.'"

19 "And he said likewise to him, 'Be thou also over five cities.'"

20 "And another came, saying, 'Lord, behold, here is thy pound, which I have kept laid up in a napkin:'"

21 "'For I feared thee, because thou art an austere man: thou takest up that thou layedst not down, and reapest that thou didst not sow.'"

22 "And he saith unto him, 'Out of thine own mouth will I judge thee, thou wicked servant. Thou knewest that I was an austere man, taking up that I laid not down, and reaping that I did not sow:'"

23 "'Wherefore then gavest not thou my money into the bank, that at my coming I might have required mine own with usury?'"

24 "And he said unto them that stood by, 'Take from him the pound, and give it to him that hath ten pounds.'"

25 "(And they said unto him, 'Lord, he hath ten pounds.')"

26 "'For I say unto you, That unto every one which hath shall be given; and from him that hath not, even that he hath shall be taken away from him.'"

27 "'But those mine enemies, which would not that I should reign over them, bring hither, and slay them before me.'"

The Ascent to the Temple

28 And when he had thus spoken, he went before, ascending up to Jerusalem.

45 And he went into the temple, and began to cast out them that sold therein, and them that bought;

46 Saying unto them, "It is written, My house is the house of prayer: but ye have made it a den of thieves."

47 And he taught daily in the temple. But the chief priests and the scribes and the chief of the people sought to destroy him,

48 And could not find what they might do: for all the people were very attentive to hear him.

Chapter XIX Notes

Zacchaeus: Severing the Anchor of Flesh (Verses 1–10) *"This day is salvation come to this house."*

- The Orthodox Spackle: The canonical text (Luke 19:9) adds the justifying clause: *"forasmuch as he also is a son of Abraham."* * The Forensic Excision: Following *Lectio Brevior Potior*, this clause is surgically removed. It is a blatant orthodox interpolation designed to re-attach the Anchor of Flesh.
- The Theological Reality: Salvation came to Zacchaeus not because of his Jewish DNA, but because he possessed the pneumatic curiosity and Faith to seek the Alien God. By removing the Abrahamic justification, the text clarifies that the "Salvation" Jesus brings is universal, unmerited, and totally disconnected from the biological Covenant of the Creator. Zacchaeus is saved *despite* his lineage and his occupation, not because of it.

The Missing Triumphal Entry: Severing the Anchor of Prophecy (Between Verses 28–45)

- The Gap: Between the ascent to Jerusalem and the entry into the Temple, there is a massive, deliberate excision. The entire canonical sequence of Jesus riding a donkey amidst crowds waving palm branches and shouting *"Blessed be the King"* and *"Son of David"* is gone.
- The Trap: The "Triumphal Entry" was the proto-orthodox church's most heavy-handed attempt to force the Alien Christ to fulfill the Anchor of Prophecy—specifically Zechariah 9:9 (*"Behold, thy King cometh... riding upon an ass"*).
- The Restoration: In the *Evangelion*, Jesus does not enter as a prophesied Jewish King coming to claim His earthly capital. He arrives abruptly, without fanfare, as an unknown, hostile Inspector walking directly into the Creator's headquarters to condemn a failing institution.

The Parable of the Pounds: The Austere Demiurge (Verses 11–27) Orthodox readers mistakenly assume the "Nobleman" is Jesus. Marcionites understood this parable as a chilling, accurate description of the Creator.

- Austeros vs. Chrestos: The servant accurately describes the master as *"an austere man"* (*austeros*—harsh, strict, drying). This stands in absolute ontological opposition to the Alien God, who is known in Marcionite theology as *Chrestos* (Kind/Good/Merciful).
- The Transactional Economy: The "Nobleman" represents the Creator God—a deity of strict accounting, merciless harvest, and legalistic judgment. He demands "usury" (works of the Law) and proudly *"reaps where he did not sow"* (claiming ownership over pneumatic souls that actually belong to the Alien Spirit).
- The Verdict of the Sword: Jesus tells this parable to illustrate the deadly reality of the system the disciples are trapped in. The Creator is a God who literally commands His enemies to be *"slain before him"* (Verse 27). The Alien God brings unmerited Life; the Creator brings the transactional Sword.

The Temple Cleansing: Evicting the Creator's Economy (Verses 45–48) *"My house is the house of prayer: but ye have made it a den of thieves."*

- The Reclamation of the Sacred: Jesus does not call it "My House" to claim architectural ownership of the Creator's stone building, but to assert Superior Authority over the very concept of the Sacred.
- The Thieves: The "thieves" are not merely the low-level money changers; they are the High Priests, the scribes, and the systemic agents of the Creator. They have turned the spiritual potential of humanity into a grotesque, material transaction of animal blood and earthly coin.
- The Judgment: The Alien Son enters the Creator's stronghold not to inhabit it, but to halt its machinery and evict its operators. He reclaims the space for pure, pneumatic prayer (the domain of the Alien God) and condemns the "den" of material sacrifice (the domain of the Demiurge).

CHAPTER XX

The Authority of Jesus Questioned

1 And it came to pass, that on one of those days, as he taught the people in the temple, and preached the gospel, the chief priests and the scribes came upon him with the elders,

2 And spake unto him, saying, "Tell us, by what authority doest thou these things? or who is he that gave thee this authority?"

3 And he answered and said unto them, "I will also ask you one thing; and answer me:"

4 "The baptism of John, was it from heaven, or of men?"

5 And they reasoned with themselves, saying, "If we shall say, From heaven; he will say, Why then believed ye him not?"

6 "But and if we say, Of men; all the people will stone us: for they be persuaded that John was a prophet."

7 And they answered, that they could not tell whence it was.

8 And Jesus said unto them, "Neither tell I you by what authority I do these things."

Paying Tribute to Caesar

19 And the chief priests and the scribes the same hour sought to lay hands on him; and they feared the people: for they perceived that he had spoken this parable against them.

20 And they watched him, and sent forth spies, which should feign themselves just men, that they might take hold of his words, that so they might deliver him unto the power and authority of the governor.

21 And they asked him, saying, "Master, we know that thou sayest and teachest rightly, neither acceptest thou the person of any, but teachest the way of God truly:"

22 "Is it lawful for us to give tribute unto Caesar, or no?"

23 But he perceived their craftiness, and said unto them, "Why tempt ye me?"

24 "Show me a penny. Whose image and superscription hath it?" They answered and said, "Caesar's."

25 And he said unto them, "Render therefore unto Caesar the things which be Caesar's, and unto God the things which be God's."

26 And they could not take hold of his words before the people: and they marveled at his answer, and held their peace.

The Question of the Resurrection

27 Then came to him certain of the Sadducees, which deny that there is any resurrection; and they asked him,

28 Saying, "Master, Moses wrote unto us, If any man's brother die, having a wife, and he die without children, that his brother should take his wife, and raise up seed unto his brother."

29 "There were therefore seven brethren: and the first took a wife, and died without children."

30 "And the second took her to wife, and he died childless."

31 "And the third took her; and in like manner the seven also: and they left no children, and died."

32 "Last of all the woman died also."

33 "Therefore in the resurrection whose wife of them is she? for seven had her to wife."

34 And Jesus answering said unto them, "The children of this world marry, and are given in marriage:"

35 "But they which shall be accounted worthy to obtain that world, and the resurrection from the dead, neither marry, nor are given in marriage:"

36 "Neither can they die any more: for they are equal unto the angels; and are the children of God, being the children of the resurrection."

38 "For he is not a God of the dead, but of the living: for all live unto him."

Christ is Not the Son of David

39 Then certain of the scribes answering said, "Master, thou hast well said."

40 And after that they durst not ask him any question at all.

41 And he said unto them, "How say they that Christ is David's son?"

42 "And David himself saith in the book of Psalms, The Lord said unto my Lord, Sit thou on my right hand,"

43 "Till I make thine enemies thy footstool."

44 "David therefore calleth him Lord, how is he then his son?"

Warning Against the Scribes

45 Then in the audience of all the people he said unto his disciples,

46 "Beware of the scribes, which desire to walk in long robes, and love greetings in the markets, and the highest seats in the synagogues, and the chief rooms at feasts;"

47 "Which devour widows' houses, and for a show make long prayers: the same shall receive greater damnation."

Chapter XX Notes

The Authority Question: Jurisdictional Immunity (Verses 1–8)

- The Interrogation: The chief priests and scribes (the wardens of the Creator's religion) demand to know Jesus's credentials. They operate in a closed system of legal authority and want to know where He falls in the Demiurge's hierarchy.
- The Trap of John: Jesus uses the baptism of John to trap them, but forensically, His refusal to answer is the true revelation.
- Sovereign Immunity: By declaring, *"Neither tell I you by what authority I do these things,"* the Alien God claims absolute jurisdictional immunity. He refuses to submit His credentials to the agents of the Creator because He operates from a higher, completely foreign Pleroma. He owes them no explanation.

The Wicked Tenants: Rejecting the Landlord's History (Excised Parable, Luke 20:9–19)

- The Orthodox Spackle: The canonical text inserts the Parable of the Wicked Tenants here, where a "Landowner" sends his servants (the prophets) and finally his son to a vineyard.
- The Forensic Excision: Following *Lectio Brevior Potior*, this is a massive orthodox interpolation designed to enforce the Anchor of Prophecy.
- The Contradiction: If retained, this parable portrays the Father of Jesus as the "Landowner" of Israel who sent the Old Testament prophets. This violently contradicts the core Marcionite thesis of the *Deus Absconditus* (the Unknown God). The Alien God has no prior history with the Creator's world. The "Vineyard" (Israel) belongs entirely to the Demiurge; the Alien Son has no inheritance to claim within it.

Paying Tribute to Caesar: The Dualism of Coin (Verses 19–26)

- The Political Trap: The spies attempt to force Jesus to take a side in the Creator's geopolitical struggles. If He says "yes," He validates Roman oppression; if He says "no," He is a political rebel against the State.
- The Economic Detachment: Jesus asks for a penny and points to the image of Caesar. He declares: *"Render therefore unto Caesar the things which be Caesar's, and unto God the things which be God's."*
- The Marcionite Implication: This is not a lesson on civic duty; it is a declaration of total cosmic dualism. The material world, its politics, and its economy (the coin) belong to the Archons (Caesar/the Demiurge). Give the material trash back to its owner. The Spirit, however, bears the image of the Alien God and must be rendered to Him. Complete detachment is required.

The Question of the Resurrection: Severing the Anchor of Flesh (Verses 27–38) The Sadducees attempt to trap Jesus using the ultimate biological law of the Creator: Levirate marriage (Deuteronomy 25), designed to endlessly propagate the flesh.

- The Trap of Biology: The scenario of the seven brothers fighting over one wife in the afterlife presupposes that the Kingdom of God is just an eternal continuation of the Creator's biological reproductive cycle.
- Encratism and the Angelic State (Verse 35): Jesus shatters the Anchor of Flesh. He declares that the children of *this* world marry, but those worthy of the *next* world *"neither marry, nor are given in marriage."*
- The Present Ethic: For Marcionites, this was not just a description of the afterlife; it was an urgent mandate for the present. To be "worthy" of the Alien Kingdom, the pneumatic believer must adopt the angelic state of celibacy *now*, actively breaking the Creator's cycle of reproduction and death.

The Great Omission: The Burning Bush (Between Verses 37–38)

- The Deletion: In the canonical text (Luke 20:37), Jesus validates the resurrection by quoting Moses at the burning bush (*"Even Moses shewed at the bush..."*). This is excised entirely.
- The Rationale: The God who spoke from the fire to Moses is the Demiurge—a god of localized geography, tribal covenants, and fire. To link the life-giving resurrection of the Alien God to the patriarchs of the Old God is a fundamental orthodox error. The true proof of the resurrection lies in the eternal nature of the Spirit, not in the dusty legal history of the Exodus.

Christ is Not the Son of David: Destroying the Bloodline (Verses 41–44) This is the Marcionite Keystone for the identity of Christ, executing the final, fatal blow to both the Anchor of Flesh and the Anchor of Prophecy.

- The Argument: The Scribes (and the orthodox church) teach that the Messiah must be the biological *"Son of David"* to fulfill prophecy.
- The Logic Bomb: Jesus uses their own scriptures (Psalm 110) against them. If David calls the Messiah "Lord" (a superior, divine title), how can the Messiah possibly be his "son" (a biologically subordinate title)?
- The Conclusion: Jesus uses this irrefutable logic not to claim the throne of Jerusalem, but to explicitly *deny* the lineage. He is not the biological Son of David. He owes no blood, no DNA, and no loyalty to Israel's kings. He is the Son of the Alien God, descending without a genealogy.

CHAPTER XXI

The Widow's Mite

1 And he looked up, and saw the rich men casting their gifts into the treasury.

2 And he saw also a certain poor widow casting in thither two mites.

3 And he said, "Of a truth I say unto you, that this poor widow hath cast in more than they all:"

4 "For all these have of their abundance cast in unto the offerings of God: but she of her penury hath cast in all the living that she had."

The Prophecy of Destruction

5 And as some spake of the temple, how it was adorned with goodly stones and gifts, he said,

6 "As for these things which ye behold, the days will come, in the which there shall not be left one stone upon another, that shall not be thrown down."

7 And they asked him, saying, "Master, but when shall these things be? and what sign will there be when these things shall come to pass?"

8 And he said, "Take heed that ye be not deceived: for many shall come in my name, saying, 'I am Christ'; and the time draweth near: go ye not therefore after them."

9 "But when ye shall hear of wars and commotions, be not terrified: for these things must first come to pass; but the end is not by and by."

10 Then said he unto them, "Nation shall rise against nation, and kingdom against kingdom:"

11 "And great earthquakes shall be in divers places, and famines, and pestilences; and fearful sights and great signs shall there be from heaven."

The Persecution of the Faithful

12 "But before all these, they shall lay their hands on you, and persecute you, delivering you up to the synagogues, and into prisons, being brought before kings and rulers for my name's sake."

13 "And it shall turn to you for a testimony."

14 "Settle it therefore in your hearts, not to meditate before what ye shall answer:"

15 "For I will give you a mouth and wisdom, which all your adversaries shall not be able to gainsay nor resist."

16 "And ye shall be betrayed both by parents, and brethren, and kinsfolks, and friends; and some of you shall they cause to be put to death."

17 "And ye shall be hated of all men for my name's sake."

18 "But there shall not an hair of your head perish."

19 "In your patience possess ye your souls."

The Vengeance of the Creator (Jerusalem's Fall)

20 "And when ye shall see Jerusalem compassed with armies, then know that the desolation thereof is nigh."

21 "Then let them which are in Judaea flee to the mountains; and let them which are in the midst of it depart out; and let not them that are in the countries enter thereinto."

22 "For these be the days of vengeance, that all things which are written may be fulfilled."

23 "But woe unto them that are with child, and to them that give suck, in those days! for there shall be great distress in the land, and wrath upon this people."

24 "And they shall fall by the edge of the sword, and shall be led away captive into all nations: and Jerusalem shall be trodden down of the Gentiles, until the times of the Gentiles be fulfilled."

The Coming of the Son of Man

25 "And there shall be signs in the sun, and in the moon, and in the stars; and upon the earth distress of nations, with perplexity; the sea and the waves roaring;"

26 "Men's hearts failing them for fear, and for looking after those things which are coming on the earth: for the powers of heaven shall be shaken."

27 "And then shall they see the Son of man coming in a cloud with power and great glory."

28 "And when these things begin to come to pass, then look up, and lift up your heads; for your redemption draweth nigh."

The Parable of the Fig Tree

29 And he spake to them a parable; "Behold the fig tree, and all the trees;"

30 "When they now shoot forth, ye see and know of your own selves that summer is now nigh at hand."

31 "So likewise ye, when ye see these things come to pass, know ye that the kingdom of God is nigh at hand."

32 "Verily I say unto you, This generation shall not pass away, till all be fulfilled."

33 "Heaven and earth shall pass away: but my words shall not pass away."

Watchfulness

34 "And take heed to yourselves, lest at any time your hearts be overcharged with surfeiting, and drunkenness, and cares of this life, and so that day come upon you unawares."

35 "For as a snare shall it come on all them that dwell on the face of the whole earth."

36 "Watch ye therefore, and pray always, that ye may be accounted worthy to escape all these things that shall come to pass, and to stand before the Son of man."

37 And in the day time he was teaching in the temple; and at night he went out, and abode in the mount that is called the mount of Olives.

38 And all the people came early in the morning to him in the
temple, for to hear him.

Chapter XXI Notes

The Tragedy of the Widow: The Devouring Economy (Verses 1–4) While orthodox tradition sentimentally reads this as a model of piety, a forensic analysis reveals this scene as a devastating indictment of the Creator's economic and religious system.

- The Devouring Temple: The Creator's House does not feed the poor; it consumes them. The widow of her penury has cast in all the living she had. She sacrifices her very survival to a stone building that Jesus immediately sentences to total annihilation in the very next breath.
- The Verdict: Her sacrifice is not a commendation; it is a crime scene. It is the ultimate proof that the Law of the Creator demands absolute material surrender and gives nothing back but stones that shall be thrown down.

"Many Shall Come in My Name": The Prophetic Trap (Verse 8) Jesus warns not just against random impostors, but against the Jewish Expectation itself.

- The Distinction: The nation was expecting a "Christ"—a political, Davidic King to conquer Rome and restore their borders. Jesus explicitly warns His followers that when men come saying, "I am Christ," they must not follow them.
- The Trap: The Alien Savior is not the Messiah of the Law. Any figure who rises to claim political power, territory, or national liberation is an agent of the Demiurge, not the Father. To follow a political "Christ" is to fall back into the Creator's geopolitical timeline.

Severing the Anchor of Flesh: Betrayal and Biology (Verses 16, 23) This chapter contains two of the most explicit warnings against the biological traps of the Creator.

- The Treason of DNA (Verse 16): Jesus warns that believers shall be betrayed by parents, brethren, kinsfolks, and friends. This is the dark reality of the Anchor of Flesh. The biological family—the very foundation of the Creator's world—will act as the immune system of the Demiurge, actively hunting down and betraying the pneumatic Spirit to the authorities.
- The Tragedy of Reproduction (Verse 23): Jesus declares a specific woe unto them that are with child, and to them that give suck in those days. In Marcionite Encratism, this is not merely a statement of pity for fleeing refugees; it is a theological warning. Those who participate in the Creator's cycle of biological reproduction tether themselves to a physical world that is earmarked for wrath and destruction.

"Days of Vengeance": The Creator's Self-Sabotage (Verses 20–24)

- The Theological Distinction: The text explicitly characterizes the fall of Jerusalem and the distress in the land as days of vengeance and wrath upon the people. The Alien God is a God of Grace and does not take vengeance. The Creator God of the Old Testament is exclusively the God of Justice, Retribution, and Vengeance.
- The Conclusion: Therefore, the violent destruction of Jerusalem by armies is the Creator punishing His own people for their failures under His strict Law. Jesus observes the impending destruction but does not orchestrate it; He is the Alien witness to the Demiurge's violent self-sabotage.

The Parable of the Fig Tree: The Barometer of Judgment (Verses 29–31) In the language of the Old Testament prophets, the Fig Tree is the ultimate symbol of National Israel and the Law.

- The Warning: Jesus uses the Fig Tree not as a symbol of spiritual hope, but as a barometer of material danger. When the trees shoot forth, it signals that summer is nigh at hand. Summer represents the scorching heat of the Creator's final judgment.
- The Resurgence: The nationalistic revival of the Creator's chosen people is not a sign of the Kingdom's triumph on earth; it is the ultimate distress signal that the final catastrophe of the material cosmos has arrived.

The Cosmological Severance (Verse 33) *"Heaven and earth shall pass away:* but *my words shall not pass away."*

- No Renewal: Unlike the orthodox, Judaic hope for a "Renewed Earth" or a physical paradise, the text promises the absolute, unmitigated obliteration of the material cosmos (Heaven and Earth).
- The Escape: The goal of the Alien God is not to fix, reform, or save the broken material world, but to extract the Spirit from it before it burns. When the sky and the earth—the prison constructed by the Demiurge—finally dissolve, only the pneumatic reality of the Alien God ("My Words") will remain as the lifeboat for the soul.

CHAPTER XXII

The Conspiracy and Preparation

1 Now the feast of unleavened bread drew nigh, which is called the Passover.

2 And the chief priests and scribes sought how they might kill him; for they feared the people.

3 Then entered Satan into Judas surnamed Iscariot, being of the number of the twelve.

4 And he went his way, and communed with the chief priests and captains, how he might betray him unto them.

5 And they were glad, and covenanted to give him money.

6 And he promised, and sought opportunity to betray him unto them in the absence of the multitude.

7 Then came the day of unleavened bread.

8 And he sent Peter and John, saying, "Go and prepare us that we may eat."

9 And they said unto him, "Where wilt thou that we prepare?"

10 And he said unto them, "Behold, when ye are entered into the city, there shall a man meet you, bearing a pitcher of water; follow him into the house where he entereth in."

11 "And ye shall say unto the goodman of the house, 'The Master saith unto thee, Where is the guestchamber, where I shall eat with my disciples?'"

12 "And he shall shew you a large upper room furnished: there make ready."

13 And they went, and found as he had said unto them: and they made ready.

The Last Supper (The Anti-Passover)

14 And when the hour was come, he sat down, and the twelve apostles with him.

15 And he said unto them, "Have I with desire desired to eat this passover with you before I suffer?"

16 "I say unto you, I will not eat thereof, until it be fulfilled in the kingdom of God."

17 And he took the cup, and gave thanks, and said, "Take this, and divide it among yourselves:"

18 "For I say unto you, I will not drink of the fruit of the vine, until the kingdom of God shall come."

19 And he took bread, and gave thanks, and brake it, and gave unto them, saying, "This is my body which is given for you: this do in remembrance of me."

20 Likewise also the cup after supper, saying, "This cup is the new testament in my blood, which is shed for you."

21 "But, behold, the hand of him that betrayeth me is with me on the table."

22 "And truly the Son of man goeth, as it was determined: but woe unto that man by whom he is betrayed!"

23 And they began to inquire among themselves, which of them it was that should do this thing.

The Dispute on Greatness

24 And there was also a strife among them, which of them should be accounted the greatest.

25 And he said unto them, "The kings of the Gentiles exercise lordship over them; and they that exercise authority upon them are called benefactors."

26 "But ye shall not be so: but he that is greatest among you, let him be as the younger; and he that is chief, as he that doth serve."

27 "For whether is greater, he that sitteth at meat, or he that serveth? is not he that sitteth at meat? but I am among you as he that serveth."

28 "Ye are they which have continued with me in my temptations."

29 "And I appoint unto you a kingdom, as my Father hath appointed unto me;"

30 "That ye may eat and drink at my table in my kingdom."

The Prediction of Peter's Denial

31 And the Lord said, "Simon, Simon, behold, Satan hath desired to have you, that he may sift you as wheat:"

32 "But I have prayed for thee, that thy faith fail not: and when thou art converted, strengthen thy brethren."

33 And he said unto him, "Lord, I am ready to go with thee, both into prison, and to death."

34 And he said, "I tell thee, Peter, the cock shall not crow this day, before that thou shalt thrice deny that thou knowest me."

The Two Swords

35 And he said unto them, "When I sent you without purse, and scrip, and shoes, lacked ye any thing?" And they said, "Nothing."

36 Then said he unto them, "But now, he that hath a purse, let him take it, and likewise his scrip: and he that hath no sword, let him sell his garment, and buy one."

37 "For I say unto you, that this that is written must yet be accomplished in me, 'And he was reckoned among the transgressors': for the things concerning me have an end."

38 And they said, "Lord, behold, here are two swords." And he said unto them, "It is enough."

The Arrest

39 And he came out, and went, as he was wont, to the mount of Olives; and his disciples also followed him.

40 And when he was at the place, he said unto them, "Pray that ye enter not into temptation."

41 And he was withdrawn from them about a stone's cast, and kneeled down, and prayed,

42 Saying, "Father, if thou be willing, remove this cup from me: nevertheless not my will, but thine, be done."

45 And when he rose up from prayer, and was come to his disciples, he found them sleeping for sorrow,

46 And said unto them, "Why sleep ye? rise and pray, lest ye enter into temptation."

47 And while he yet spake, behold a multitude, and he that was called Judas, one of the twelve, went before them, and drew near unto Jesus to kiss him.

48 But Jesus said unto him, "Judas, betrayest thou the Son of man with a kiss?"

49 When they which were about him saw what would follow, they said unto him, "Lord, shall we smite with the sword?"

50 And one of them smote the servant of the high priest, and cut off his right ear.

51 And Jesus answered and said, "Suffer ye thus far." And he touched his ear, and healed him.

52 Then Jesus said unto the chief priests, and captains of the temple, and the elders, which were come to him, "Be ye come out, as against a thief, with swords and staves?"

53 "When I was daily with you in the temple, ye stretched forth no hands against me: but this is your hour, and the power of darkness."

Peter's Denial

54 Then took they him, and led him, and brought him into the high priest's house. And Peter followed afar off.

55 And when they had kindled a fire in the midst of the hall, and were set down together, Peter sat down among them.

56 But a certain maid beheld him as he sat by the fire, and earnestly looked upon him, and said, "This man was also with him."

57 And he denied him, saying, "Woman, I know him not."

58 And after a little while another saw him, and said, "Thou art also of them." And Peter said, "Man, I am not."

59 And about the space of one hour after another confidently affirmed, saying, "Of a truth this fellow also was with him: for he is a Galilaean."

60 And Peter said, "Man, I know not what thou sayest." And immediately, while he yet spake, the cock crew.

61 And the Lord turned, and looked upon Peter. And Peter remembered the word of the Lord, how he had said unto him, "Before the cock crow, thou shalt deny me thrice."

62 And Peter went out, and wept bitterly.

The Mocking and The Trial

63 And the men that held Jesus mocked him, and smote him.

64 And when they had blindfolded him, they struck him on the face, and asked him, saying, "Prophesy, who is it that smote thee?"

65 And many other things blasphemously spake they against him.

66 And as soon as it was day, the elders of the people and the chief priests and the scribes came together, and led him into their council, saying,

67 "Art thou the Christ? tell us." And he said unto them, "If I tell you, ye will not believe:"

68 "And if I also ask you, ye will not answer me, nor let me go."

69 "Hereafter shall the Son of man sit on the right hand of the power of God."

70 Then said they all, "Art thou then the Son of God?" And he said unto them, "Ye say that I am."

71 And they said, "What need we any further witness? for we ourselves have heard of his own mouth."

Chapter XXII Notes

The Anti-Passover: Hijacking the Creator's Ritual (Verses 14–20)

- The Negative Passover (Verse 15): The canonical text reads this as a positive statement. However, Epiphanius (*Panarion 42*) explicitly testifies that Marcionites read this as a negative rhetorical question: *"Have I with desire desired to eat this passover before I suffer?"* (Meaning: *I have absolutely no desire to eat this.*)
- Severing the Anchor of Prophecy: Marcion needed to violently break the link between the Last Supper and the Jewish Passover. The Passover is the Creator's foundational rite, commemorating the Exodus and the retributive slaughter of the Egyptian firstborn. By refusing the Passover lamb, Jesus hijacks the event, replacing the "Old Covenant" of animal blood and tribal vengeance with the "New Testament" of the Alien Spirit.

The Great Omission: The Thrones of Israel (Verse 30)

- The Orthodox Spackle: The canonical text (Luke 22:30) ends this verse with the promise that the disciples will *"sit on thrones judging the twelve tribes of Israel."* This clause is surgically removed.
- The Bureaucratic Voice: This is the ultimate example of the "Ecclesiastical Voice" you outlined in the preface. To promise the disciples "thrones" over the "twelve tribes" is to validate the very political and legal system Jesus came to dissolve. It implies the goal of the Gospel is to become the new management of the Demiurge's kingdom.
- The Marcionite Separation: By cutting this clause, the promise remains purely pneumatic: communion at the Alien Father's table. The Kingdom is a state of being, not a geopolitical court of law. The Alien God does not judge Israel; He ignores it.

The Two Swords: The Disciples' Blindness (Verses 35–38)

- The Misunderstanding: Jesus is speaking metaphorically about the impending hostility of the Creator's world. The disciples, still hopelessly tethered to the material realm, literally produce two physical swords (the tools of the Creator).
- "It is Enough": When Jesus says *"It is enough"* (*hikanon estin*), He is not confirming their armory. In the Marcionite reading, this is a sharp sigh of resignation and dismissal. It means: *"Enough of this conversation; you are entirely missing the point."*

Textual Restoration: The Excision of the Bloody Sweat (Verses 43–44)

- The Text: The canonical verses depicting an angel strengthening Jesus and His sweat becoming *"as it were great drops of blood"* are completely excised.
- The Forensic Rationale: Even modern canonical scholarship recognizes these verses as a later, clumsy interpolation. For the Marcionite reconstruction, they are doubly rejected. They were injected by the orthodox editors to enforce the Anchor of Flesh—forcing Jesus to exhibit a biological terror of death and a physical body capable of sweating blood. This violently contradicts the Pauline/Marcionite docetic view of the Savior as pure, descending Spirit.

The Arrest: The Power of Darkness (Verses 47–53)

- The Healing of the Ear: When the disciple violently cuts off the ear of the High Priest's servant, Jesus says, *"Suffer ye thus far,"* and immediately heals the enemy. Even in the moment of His arrest, the Alien God interrupts the Demiurge's cycle of violence (*Lex Talionis*) with unmerited Grace.
- The Surrender to the Archons: Jesus explicitly defines the jurisdiction of the arresting mob: *"This is your hour, and the power of darkness."* He recognizes that He has willingly stepped into the fatal machinery of the Creator's legal system.

The Failure of the Pillar: Peter's Denial (Verses 54–62)

- The Destruction of the Orthodox Hierarchy: Paul's "Authentic Voice" was constantly at war with the Jerusalem establishment. This sequence proves it. Peter—the supposed Rock of the orthodox church—completely fails.
- The Contrast: While the Alien Christ stands firm against the High Priests of the Creator, Peter cowers before a servant girl. The narrative proves that the original disciples were entirely too weak and biologically terrified to be trusted with the true Gospel, underlining the direct revelation to Paul.

The Trial: Rejecting the Title (Verses 66–71)

- The Ambiguity of the Messiah: The elders demand, *"Art thou the Christ?"* Jesus completely refuses to claim the title of the Jewish Messiah. He answers: *"If I tell you, ye will not believe."*
- "Ye Say That I Am": When they ask if He is the Son of God, He throws their own words back at them: *"Ye say that I am."* He refuses to let the Creator's priests define His ontology. He goes to the cross incognito, unrecognized by the rulers of this age.

CHAPTER XXIII

The Trial Before Pilate

1 And the whole multitude of them arose, and led him unto Pilate.

2 And they began to accuse him, saying, "We found this fellow perverting the nation, and forbidding to give tribute to Caesar, and saying that he himself is Christ a King."

2b "And he destroyeth the law and the prophets."

3 And Pilate asked him, saying, "Art thou the King of the Jews?" And he answered him and said, "Thou sayest it."

4 Then said Pilate to the chief priests and to the people, "I find no fault in this man."

5 And they were the more fierce, saying, "He stirreth up the people, teaching throughout all Jewry, beginning from Galilee to this place."

The Trial Before Herod

6 When Pilate heard of Galilee, he asked whether the man were a Galilaean.

7 And as soon as he knew that he belonged unto Herod's jurisdiction, he sent him to Herod, who himself also was at Jerusalem at that time.

8 And when Herod saw Jesus, he was exceeding glad: for he was desirous to see him of a long season, because he had heard many

things of him; and he hoped to have seen some miracle done by him.

9 Then he questioned with him in many words; but he answered him nothing.

10 And the chief priests and scribes stood and vehemently accused him.

11 And Herod with his men of war set him at nought, and mocked him, and arrayed him in a gorgeous robe, and sent him again to Pilate.

The Sentence

13 And Pilate, when he had called together the chief priests and the rulers and the people,

14 Said unto them, "Ye have brought this man unto me, as one that perverteth the people: and, behold, I, having examined him before you, have found no fault in this man touching those things whereof ye accuse him:"

15 "No, nor yet Herod: for I sent you to him; and, lo, nothing worthy of death is done unto him."

16 "I will therefore chastise him, and release him."

18 And they cried out all at once, saying, "Away with this man, and release unto us Barabbas:"

19 (Who for a certain sedition made in the city, and for murder, was cast into prison.)

20 Pilate therefore, willing to release Jesus, spake again to them.

21 But they cried, saying, "Crucify him, crucify him."

22 And he said unto them the third time, "Why, what evil hath he done? I have found no cause of death in him: I will therefore chastise him, and let him go."

23 And they were instant with loud voices, requiring that he might be crucified. And the voices of them and of the chief priests prevailed.

24 And Pilate gave sentence that it should be as they required.

25 And he released unto them him that for sedition and murder was cast into prison, whom they had desired; but he delivered Jesus to their will.

The Road to Calvary

26 And as they led him away, they laid hold upon one Simon, a Cyrenian, coming out of the country, and on him they laid the cross, that he might bear it after Jesus.

27 And there followed him a great company of people, and of women, which also bewailed and lamented him.

28 But Jesus turning unto them said, "Daughters of Jerusalem, weep not for me, but weep for yourselves, and for your children."

29 "For, behold, the days are coming, in the which they shall say, 'Blessed are the barren, and the wombs that never bare, and the paps which never gave suck.'"

30 "Then shall they begin to say to the mountains, 'Fall on us'; and to the hills, 'Cover us.'"

31 "For if they do these things in a green tree, what shall be done in the dry?"

The Crucifixion

32 And there were also two other, malefactors, led with him to be put to death.

33 And when they were come to the place, which is called Calvary, there they crucified him, and the malefactors, one on the right hand, and the other on the left.

34 Then said Jesus, "Father, forgive them; for they know not what they do." And they parted his raiment, and cast lots.

35 And the people stood beholding. And the rulers also with them derided him, saying, "He saved others; let him save himself, if he be Christ, the chosen of God."

36 And the soldiers also mocked him, coming to him, and offering him vinegar,

37 And saying, "If thou be the king of the Jews, save thyself."

38 And a superscription also was written over him in letters of Greek, and Latin, and Hebrew, THIS IS THE KING OF THE JEWS.

The Two Thieves

39 And one of the malefactors which were hanged railed on him, saying, "If thou be Christ, save thyself and us."

40 But the other answering rebuked him, saying, "Dost not thou fear God, seeing thou art in the same condemnation?"

41 "And we indeed justly; for we receive the due reward of our deeds: but this man hath done nothing amiss."

42 And he said unto Jesus, "Lord, remember me when thou comest into thy kingdom."

43 And Jesus said unto him, "Verily I say unto you, To day shalt thou be with me in paradise."

The Death

44 And it was about the sixth hour, and there was a darkness over all the earth until the ninth hour.

45 And the sun was darkened, and the veil of the temple was rent in the midst.

46 And when Jesus had cried with a loud voice, he said, "Father, into thy hands I commend my spirit": and having said thus, he gave up the ghost.

47 Now when the centurion saw what was done, he glorified God, saying, "Certainly this was a righteous man."

48 And all the people that came together to that sight, beholding the things which were done, smote their breasts, and returned.

49 And all his acquaintance, and the women that followed him from Galilee, stood afar off, beholding these things.

The Burial

50 And, behold, there was a man named Joseph, a counsellor; and he was a good man, and a just:

51 (The same had not consented to the counsel and deed of them;) he was of Arimathaea, a city of the Jews: who also himself waited for the kingdom of God.

52 This man went unto Pilate, and begged the body of Jesus.

53 And he took it down, and wrapped it in linen, and laid it in a sepulchre that was hewn in stone, wherein never man before was laid.

54 And that day was the preparation, and the sabbath drew on.

55 And the women also, which came with him from Galilee, followed after, and beheld the sepulchre, and how his body was laid.

56 And they returned, and prepared spices and ointments; and rested the sabbath day according to the commandment.

Chapter XXIII Notes

The True Indictment: "He Destroyeth the Law" (Verses 1–2b)

- The Frame-Up: The multitude rose up, led Jesus to Pilate, and accused Him of perverting the nation, forbidding tribute to Caesar, and claiming to be Christ a King. The Jewish leaders know He is not their prophesied, militaristic Messiah. To execute Him, they must translate His spiritual threat into the Creator's political language (sedition).
- The Marcionite Variant (Verse 2b): The text explicitly includes the charge: *"And he destroyeth the law and the prophets"*. While orthodox editors excised this from canonical manuscripts, Epiphanius reports Marcion retained it.
- The Forensic Truth: In the canonical view, this is a lie told by the Jews to trick Pilate. In the Marcionite forensic reading, *it is the absolute truth*. Jesus actually did come to dissolve the Creator's Law and terminate the prophets. The religious authorities correctly identified the Alien God as an existential threat to their system.

The Jurisdictional Silence: Pilate and Herod (Verses 3–11)

- "Thou Sayest It" (Verse 3): When Pilate directly asks if He is the King of the Jews, Jesus responds only with, *"Thou sayest it"*. He refuses to step into the role of the Jewish Messiah or claim a title that belongs to the Creator's geopolitical timeline.
- The Silence Before the Tetrarch (Verse 9): Pilate sent Jesus to Herod's jurisdiction, where Herod questioned Him in many words, but Jesus answered him nothing. The Alien God flatly refuses to defend Himself before the bureaucratic managers of the Demiurge. He owes no explanation to the rulers of this age.

Severing the Anchor of Flesh: "Blessed are the Barren" (Verses 27–31)

- The Reversal of Genesis: As women bewailed and lamented Him, Jesus turned and told the "Daughters of Jerusalem" not to weep for Him, but for themselves and their children.
- The Ascetic Command (Verse 29): He prophesies that days are coming when people will say, *"Blessed are the barren, and the wombs that never bare, and the paps which never gave suck"*. The Creator's first biological command was "Be fruitful and multiply." The Alien Christ completely reverses this. He frames the cessation of biological reproduction (the Anchor of Flesh) as a supreme blessing, because reproducing only feeds more souls into a material world destined for destruction.

The Crucifixion: Grace vs. Lex Talionis (Verses 32–43)

- The Ultimate Distinction (Verse 34): While being crucified, Jesus says, *"Father, forgive them; for they know not what they do"*. The Creator God of the Old Testament demands an eye for an eye and visits the sins of the fathers upon the children. The Alien Father forgives the ultimate crime (Deicide) because it is committed in the ignorance of the material world.
- The Superscription (Verse 38): A superscription was written over Him in Greek, Latin, and Hebrew: *"THIS IS THE KING OF THE JEWS"*. This is the final, desperate attempt by the Material World to enforce the Anchor of Prophecy. The Archons try to pin the Cosmic Christ to a specific ethnicity and history, labeling the pure Spirit with a tribal name.
- The Bankruptcy of the Law (Verses 39-43): One malefactor demands Jesus save Himself and them, but the other rebukes him, noting that they receive the *"due reward"* of their deeds, while Jesus has done nothing amiss. The second thief acknowledges the strict, retributive justice of the Creator (due reward). He simply asks Jesus to remember him. Jesus immediately responds, *"To day shalt thou be with me in paradise"*. Jesus grants salvation instantly, completely bypassing the Creator's legal requirements for Temple sacrifice or atonement.

The Death of the Stranger: Rending the Veil (Verses 44–49)

- The Cosmic Rupture (Verse 45): At the sixth hour, darkness covered the earth, the sun was darkened, and the veil of the temple was rent in the midst.
- The Exposure of the Demiurge: For Marcionites, this was not just a sign of mourning. The veil functioned to protect the Creator's Holy of Holies from the world. By tearing it from the inside out, the Alien God violently breaks the separation, exposing the utter emptiness of the Creator's house. The "Mystery" of the Jewish God is terminated.
- The Extraction (Verse 46): Jesus cried with a loud voice, *"Father, into thy hands I commend my spirit,"* and gave up the ghost. He leaves the biological flesh—the garment of the Creator—hanging on the wood, and extracts the Spirit back to the Pleroma.

CHAPTER XXIV

The Empty Tomb

1 Now upon the first day of the week, very early in the morning, they came unto the sepulchre, bringing the spices which they had prepared, and certain others with them.

2 And they found the stone rolled away from the sepulchre.

3 And they entered in, and found not the body of the Lord Jesus.

4 And it came to pass, as they were much perplexed thereabout, behold, two men stood by them in shining garments:

5 And as they were afraid, and bowed down their faces to the earth, they said unto them, "Why seek ye the living among the dead?"

6 "He is not here, but is risen: remember how he spake unto you when he was yet in Galilee,"

7 "Saying, 'The Son of man must be delivered into the hands of sinful men, and be crucified, and the third day rise again.'"

8 And they remembered his words,

9 And returned from the sepulchre, and told all these things unto the eleven, and to all the rest.

10 It was Mary Magdalene, and Joanna, and Mary the mother of James, and other women that were with them, which told these things unto the apostles.

11 And their words seemed to them as idle tales, and they believed them not.

12 Then arose Peter, and ran unto the sepulchre; and stooping down, he beheld the linen clothes laid by themselves, and departed, wondering in himself at that which was come to pass.

The Road to Emmaus (The Unknown Stranger)

13 And, behold, two of them went that same day to a village called Emmaus, which was from Jerusalem about threescore furlongs.

14 And they talked together of all these things which had happened.

15 And it came to pass, that, while they communed together and reasoned, Jesus himself drew near, and went with them.

16 But their eyes were holden that they should not know him.

17 And he said unto them, "What manner of communications are these that ye have one to another, as ye walk, and are sad?"

18 And the one of them, whose name was Cleopas, answering said unto him, "Art thou only a stranger in Jerusalem, and hast not known the things which are come to pass there in these days?"

19 And he said unto them, "What things?" And they said unto him, "Concerning Jesus of Nazareth, which was a prophet mighty in deed and word before God and all the people:"

20 "And how the chief priests and our rulers delivered him to be condemned to death, and have crucified him."

21 "But we trusted that it had been he which should have redeemed Israel: and beside all this, to day is the third day since these things were done."

22 "Yea, and certain women also of our company made us astonished, which were early at the sepulchre;"

23 "And when they found not his body, they came, saying, that they had also seen a vision of angels, which said that he was alive."

24 "And certain of them which were with us went to the sepulchre, and found it even so as the women had said: but him they saw not."

25 Then he said unto them, "O fools, and slow of heart to believe all that I have spoken to you!"

26 "Ought not Christ to have suffered these things, and to enter into his glory?"

28 And they drew nigh unto the village, whither they went: and he made as though he would have gone further.

29 But they constrained him, saying, "Abide with us: for it is toward evening, and the day is far spent." And he went in to tarry with them.

30 And it came to pass, as he sat at meat with them, he took bread, and blessed it, and brake, and gave to them.

31 And their eyes were opened, and they knew him; and he vanished out of their sight.

32 And they said one to another, "Did not our heart burn within us, while he talked with us by the way?"

33 And they rose up the same hour, and returned to Jerusalem, and found the eleven gathered together, and them that were with them,

34 Saying, "The Lord is risen indeed, and hath appeared to Simon."

35 And they told what things were done in the way, and how he was known of them in breaking of bread.

The Appearance to the Disciples (The Phantasm)

36 And as they thus spake, Jesus himself stood in the midst of them, and saith unto them, "Peace be unto you."

37 But they were terrified and affrighted, and supposed that they had seen a spirit.

38 And he said unto them, "Why are ye troubled? and why do thoughts arise in your hearts?"

39 "Behold my hands and my feet, that it is I myself: for a spirit hath not flesh and bones, as ye see me have."

40 And when he had thus spoken, he shewed them his hands and his feet.

41 And while they yet believed not for joy, and wondered, he said unto them, "Have ye here any meat?"

42 And they gave him a piece of a broiled fish, and of an honeycomb.

43 And he took it, and did eat before them.

The Final Commission & Ascension

44 And he said unto them, "These are the words which I spake unto you, while I was yet with you, that thus it behoved Christ to suffer, and to rise from the dead the third day:"

47 "And that repentance and remission of sins should be preached in his name among all nations."

48 "And ye are witnesses of these things."

49 "And, behold, I send the promise of my Father upon you: but tarry ye in the city of Jerusalem, until ye be endued with power from on high."

50 And he led them out as far as to Bethany, and he lifted up his hands, and blessed them.

51 And it came to pass, while he blessed them, he was parted from them, and carried up into heaven.

52 And they worshipped him, and returned to Jerusalem with great joy.

Chapter XXIV Notes

"Why Seek Ye the Living Among the Dead?" (Verses 1–5) This verse became the ultimate Marcionite rallying cry.

- The Ontological Distinction: "The Living" refers exclusively to the Alien God (who is pure Life and Spirit). "The Dead" refers entirely to the Creator's material universe, which Marcionites viewed as a sprawling biological graveyard.
- The Great Escape: The women were looking for a corpse in a Jewish tomb, expecting the Alien Christ to be subject to the Demiurge's laws of biological decay. The Angels' question is a rebuke: Christ does not belong to the realm of biology. He has not merely "risen" within the system; He has completely evacuated the Creator's machinery of death.

The Emmaus Stranger and the Political Trap (Verses 13–26) The Road to Emmaus is a profound demonstration of the disciples' lingering blindness.

- The Anchor of Prophecy: Cleopas and his companion confess their dashed geopolitical hopes: *"we trusted that it had been he which should have redeemed Israel"*. Even after the resurrection, they are still trapped in the Creator's paradigm, expecting a militaristic Messiah to liberate a strip of Middle Eastern real estate.
- The Rebuke: Jesus responds, *"O fools, and slow of heart to believe all that I have spoken to you!"*. He rebukes them not for failing to read the Old Testament, but for failing to listen to *His* Alien revelation.

Severing the Anchor of Prophecy (Verses 25, 27, 44)

- The Orthodox Spackle: In Canonical Luke, the Resurrected Jesus spends significant time walking the disciples through the scriptures, explaining how His death was predicted by Moses, the Prophets, and the Psalms.

- The Forensic Excision: Marcion surgically excised all references where Jesus validates the Old Testament. Because the Alien God was entirely unknown to the Prophets, Moses could not possibly have written about Him.
- The Replacement: In the *Evangelion*, Jesus refers only to His own previous words, stating, *"These are the words which I spake unto you, while I was yet with you"*. The authority for the Resurrection comes strictly from the Son Himself, completely severing the timeline of the Jewish Scroll.

The "Flesh and Bones" Controversy: The Docetic Phantasm (Verses 36–43) Canonical Luke 24:39 is historically considered the strongest anti-Docetic verse in the New Testament (*"a spirit hath not flesh and bones"*).

- The Anthropological Conflict: Orthodox editors used this to chain Jesus back to the Anchor of Flesh. However, Marcionites strictly denied Jesus had material flesh, viewing it as the corruptible evil matter of the Demiurge.
- The Forensic Defense: Marcion famously retained the verse but interpreted it rhetorically. When the disciples are terrified, supposing they had seen a "spirit", they are thinking of a ghost or demon from the Creator's underworld (Hades). Jesus proves He is not a shadowy underworld demon, but a solid, superior manifestation of the Alien God. He is a divine "Phantasm"—real to the sight and touch, capable of interacting with the physical world (eating fish), yet completely uncorrupted by the Demiurge's biological atoms.

The Final Omission: Evacuating the Temple (Verses 50–53)

- The Canonical Cut: The canonical text (Luke 24:53) ends with the disciples returning to Jerusalem, *"continually in the temple, praising and blessing God"*.
- The Rationale: Following the *Evangelion*'s internal logic, this orthodox ending is forensically impossible. Jesus had already declared the Temple "desolate" in Chapter XIII and violently tore its veil in Chapter XXIII, signifying the absolute departure of the Divine.

- The True Conclusion: Enlightened pneumatic disciples would never return to worship in the empty, condemned house of the Creator. Therefore, the *Evangelion* ends exactly where it must: with the triumphant Ascension of the Alien God back to the Pleroma, completely severing all ties with Judaism and the material earth.

APPENDIX A: THE REDACTED FILES

A Forensic Reconstruction of the Earliest Christian Signal

CASE NOTE: The following files represent a "controlled subtraction" of the textual evidence. When the later, stylized additions—the fingerprints of subsequent orthodoxy—are lifted from the extant letters of Paul, a startlingly different profile emerges. What follows is the raw signal before the narrative static began.

EXHIBIT I: THE TAMPERED EVIDENCE

Subject: Anomalies in the Received Text
Status: Pre-Marcionite Interpolations

A forensic audit of the Greek text reveals distinct fracture points where the "voice" of the Apostle shifts. In these locations, the syntax becomes balanced, the vocabulary foreign, and the theology dangerously "safe." These are not the words of the radical mystic; they are creedal formulas inserted to anchor Paul's cosmic Christ into the mechanism of Jewish history.

A. The "Davidic" Insertion (Romans 1:3-4)

- The Received Text: *"...made of the seed of David according to the flesh..."*
- The Forensic Anomaly: This is the only instance in the entire Pauline corpus where the name "David" is linked to Jesus. Everywhere else, Paul builds his Christology exclusively on the Resurrection, never on bloodline.
- The "Tell": The structure is a symmetrical creed (Flesh vs. Spirit / Descended vs. Declared). It is likely a pre-Pauline Jewish-Christian hymn pasted into the opening salutation to legitimize Paul's message for a Jewish audience.

- The Marcionite Correction: Marcion excised this clause. In his *Apostolikon*, the text read: *"Paul, a servant of Jesus Christ, called to be an apostle, separated unto the gospel of God... concerning his Son, Jesus Christ our Lord."* Without the insertion, Jesus has no earthly genealogy.

B. The "Biological" Insertion (Galatians 4:4)

- The Received Text: *"...born of a woman, born under the law..."*
- The Forensic Anomaly: The Authentic Paul argues relentlessly that Christ is the end (*telos*) of the Law. It is theologically inconsistent for him to define the Savior's origin by the very slavery He came to abolish.
- The "Tell": "Born of a woman" is a defensive polemic. It is not a biographical detail (every human is born of a woman); it is a theological

shield raised against Docetism (the belief that Jesus was a phantom). It was inserted to force the Spirit into biological mortality.

- The Marcionite Correction: Marcion excised this phrase. His text read: *"But when the fullness of the time was come, God sent forth his Son... to redeem them that were under the Law."*

C. The "Political" Insertion (1 Thessalonians 2:14-16)

- The Received Text: *"...the Jews, who killed both the Lord Jesus and the prophets... for the wrath has come upon them at last."*
- The Forensic Anomaly: Paul died in the 60s CE. The destruction of Jerusalem (the "wrath") occurred in 70 CE. Paul could not write about a future event as if it had already happened.

- The "Tell": This passage breaks the flow of the letter and contradicts Paul's hope for Israel's salvation in Romans 11. It is a later *vaticinium ex eventu* (prophecy from the event)—a forgery inserted by the church to blame the Jews for the Roman war, absolving Rome and incriminating the biological family of Jesus.

EXHIBIT II: THE PROFILE (THE PAULINE CORE)

Subject: The Apostle's Original Testimony
Method: Subtraction of Exhibit I

When the creedal insertions are removed, the "Pauline Core" stands revealed. This is the witness statement before the story was coordinated with the Gospels.

1. The Origin is Cosmic, Not Local The Subject claims no knowledge of a Nazareth, a Bethlehem, or a historical "Ministry." The event took place in the "fullness of time" (a cosmic coordinate), not "in the days of Herod" (a historical coordinate).

2. The Antagonists were the "Archons" Paul does not describe a Jewish rabbi run afoul of the Sanhedrin. He describes a pre-existent entity ambushed by the "Princes of this World" (Gr. *Archon*) (1 Corinthians 2:8). These are not human rulers (like Pilate), but the invisible Rulers of the Age. The crucifixion was not a miscarriage of Roman justice; it was a cosmic trap sprung on the Creator's powers.

3. The Witness is Visionary Paul equates his own experience on the Damascus Road (a vision of light) with the experiences of Peter and James. He makes no distinction between "walking with him in Galilee" and "seeing him in glory." In the Core Profile, the primary evidence for the Resurrection is spectral, not physical.

4. The Silence is Deafening In this reconstructed layer, the following elements are entirely missing from the case file:

- Miracles: Zero.
- Parables: Zero.
- The Empty Tomb: Zero.
- The Trial: No Pontius Pilate, no Caiaphas, no Judas.

EXHIBIT III: THE CHAIN OF CUSTODY

Subject: The Corruption of the Signal

If Paul is "Patient Zero" of the theology, the Gospel of Mark (in its earliest layer) represents the first attempt to Historicize that theology. The following analysis tracks how the Cosmic Event was slowly dragged down to earth by later editors.

ITEM 1: THE BEGINNING

- The Pauline Core (c. 50s CE): Revelation. God reveals the Son "in" Paul.
- The Markan Historicization (c. 70 CE): Baptism. God declares the Son to John the Baptist.
- The Shift: The moment of "Sonship" is moved from the Resurrection back to a historical event.

ITEM 2: THE CONFLICT

- The Pauline Core: Cosmic. Invisible "Rulers of this Age" (*Archons*) unknowingly crucify the Lord of Glory.
- The Markan Historicization: Social. Scribes, Pharisees, and Romans conspire to kill Jesus.
- The Shift: Cosmic demons are replaced by human antagonists (The Jews/Romans).

ITEM 3: THE DEATH

- The Pauline Core: Atonement. A necessary cosmic inversion to break the Law.
- The Markan Historicization: Tragedy. A lonely cry of dereliction on a hill.
- The Shift: The theology is dramatized into a scene of suffering.

ITEM 4: THE EVIDENCE

- The Pauline Core: Scripture & Spirit. "According to the Scriptures."
- The Markan Historicization: Miracles. Public displays of power over nature.
- The Shift: Spiritual authority is converted into physical proof.

ITEM 5: THE RESURRECTION

- The Pauline Core: Appearances. He "was seen" (*ophthe*) by Cephas, then the twelve.
- The Markan Historicization: The Tomb. The women find the tomb; the body is missing.
- The Shift: A visionary encounter is converted into a "Missing Person" case.

ITEM 6: THE ENDING

- The Pauline Core: Triumph. "He must reign until he hath put all enemies under his feet."
- The Markan Historicization: Fear. "They said nothing to anyone, for they were afraid." (Mk 16:8)
- The Shift: Mark's original ending preserves the ambiguity of the Pauline silence.

APPENDIX B: FORENSIC EXHIBIT CASE FILE: THE DAMASCUS DIVERGENCE

SUBJECT: The Conversion of Paul CONFLICT: Primary Source (Paul) vs. Secondary Narrative (Acts)

EVIDENCE A: THE CHURCH NARRATIVE (Acts 9:3-19) *Source: Attributed to "Luke" (c. 85-90 A.D.)*

- The Event: Paul is blinded by a light and rendered helpless.
- The Handler: Paul is led by the hand into Damascus.
- The Submission: Paul remains blind until Ananias (a representative of the Church) lays hands on him.
- The Implication: Paul's authority is derivative. He submitted to the hierarchy to receive his sight.

EVIDENCE B: THE PAULINE TESTIMONY (Galatians 1:11-17) *Source: The Apostle Paul (c. 50-55 A.D.)*

- The Event: "God was pleased to reveal his Son in me."

- The Independence: "I did not consult with any human being."
- The Denial: "I did not go up to Jerusalem to those who were apostles before me."
- The Reality: Paul went immediately into Arabia (the desert) alone. He bypassed the Church structure entirely.

VERDICT: The Book of Acts is a political edit designed to domesticate Paul and place him under the authority of Jerusalem. The *Evangelion* restores his independent, direct connection to the Alien God.

INVESTIGATOR'S CONCLUSION

The investigation concludes that the "Original Paul" possessed a Christology of Descent and Ascent, entirely unmoored from the biographical details that later saturated the tradition.

The "Jesus of History" was not the foundation upon which Paul built. Rather, the **Christ of Faith** was the figure Paul encountered. The history was back-filled later—clues planted at the scene—to make the Cosmic Christ recognizable to a world that demanded a human story.

THE UNBROKEN SIGNAL

This is the signal stripped of the static. When the layers of history, politics, and flesh are burned away, these nineteen assertions remain. They are not merely a theology; they are the algorithm of a new consciousness. This is the Gospel before the Church invented Christianity.

I did not receive my gospel from any human being, nor was I taught it.

It came through revelation.

God revealed his Son in me.

The rulers of this age did not understand him.

If they had, they would not have crucified the Lord of glory.

We preach Christ crucified — a scandal, foolishness, weakness.

Yet this is the power of God.

The Cross destroys the wisdom of the world.

He was raised.

He appeared.

Last of all, he appeared to me.

The appointed time has grown short.

The present form of this world is passing away.

The law enslaves.

The flesh cannot inherit the kingdom.

The Spirit makes alive.

Walk by the Spirit.

You are a new creation.

Christ lives in you.

EVIDENCE LOG: PRIMARY DATASET & SCHOLARLY CORROBORATION

I. THE ANCIENT TEXTS (THE CRIME SCENE)

- *Nestle-Aland Novum Testamentum Graece (28th Edition): The standard critical text of the New Testament, used here to identify the Greek syntax of the "Ecclesiastical Voice."*
- *The Apostolikon & Evangelion: The reconstructed canon of Marcion of Sinope (c. 140 CE), as preserved in the hostile attestations of Tertullian (Adversus Marcionem), Epiphanius (Panarion), and Adamantius.*
- *Flavius Josephus, Antiquities of the Jews: Specifically Book XX, examined here for later Christian interpolations regarding "James, the brother of Jesus" and as a source plagiarized by the author of Acts.*
- *The Apostolic Fathers (Clement of Rome, Ignatius of Antioch): Analyzed here not as reliable witnesses, but as the earliest architects of the harmonization project and the manufacturing of "orthodox" authority.*

II. FORENSIC SCHOLARSHIP (CORROBORATING ANALYSIS)

A. The Reconstruction of the Marcionite Text

- *Adolf von Harnack, Marcion: Das Evangelium vom fremden Gott (1921): The foundational philological reconstruction of the Marcionite text.*
- *Dieter T. Roth, The Text of Marcion's Gospel (2015): The modern critical standard. Corrects Harnack's deficiencies and provides the most granular data on what was strictly attestable in Marcion's Evangelion.*
- *Jason BeDuhn, The First New Testament: Marcion's Scriptural Canon: Argues for the priority of Marcion's text over the canonical Luke, reversing the traditional direction of dependence.*

B. The Synoptic Problem & Marcionite Priority

- *John Knox, Marcion and the New Testament: The foundational argument that Luke-Acts was written as a direct reaction to Marcion.*
- *Matthias Klinghardt, The Oldest Gospel and the Formation of the Canonical Gospels: Provides the comprehensive academic framework establishing Marcion's Gospel as the primary source for Luke and the key to solving the Synoptic Problem.*

- *Markus Vinzent, Marcion and the Dating of the Synoptic Gospels: Establishes Marcion's Gospel as the chronological anchor and primary source for all four canonical Gospels.*

C. The "Cover-Up" Operation (Acts & The Publication Event)

- *Richard Pervo, Dating Acts (2006) & The Mystery of Acts (2008): Corroborates the late dating of Acts (c. 115-130 CE) and demonstrates its reliance on Josephus and fiction to harmonize the "Peter" and "Paul" factions.*
- *Joseph B. Tyson, Marcion and Luke-Acts: A Defining Struggle: Details the specific anti-Marcionite theological agenda of the Lukan author.*
- *David Trobisch, The First Edition of the New Testament (2000): Argues that the New Testament was not slowly "collected" but was published as a unified, edited anthology (c. 150 CE) to counter Marcion, utilizing specific editorial devices (e.g., Nomina Sacra) to unify the text.*

D. The Mechanics of Interpolation (The "Ecclesiastical Voice")

- *Winsome Munro, Authority in Paul and Peter: Identifies the "Pastoral Stratum"—a distinct layer of interpolation inserted into the authentic letters to subordinate Paul to the developing orthodox hierarchy.*

- *William O. Walker Jr., Interpolations in the Pauline Letters: Establishes the formal criteria for detecting non-Pauline insertions, providing the "fingerprints" of the Ecclesiastical Editor.*
- *J.C. O'Neill, Paul's Letter to the Romans: Identifies extensive interpolations and glosses in the received text of Paul.*
- *Hermann Detering, The Fabricated Paul: Critical analysis of the Pastoral Epistles and the Dutch Radical critique of Pauline authenticity.*

III. METHODOLOGY

- *Algorithmic Stylometry: The use of Large Language Models (LLMs) to detect variance in vocabulary density, sentence structure, and theological distinctiveness between the "Authentic" and "Ecclesiastical" layers of the text.*

ABOUT THE AUTHOR

Forth Given is the pseudonym of an information systems specialist and researcher dedicated to the intersection of ancient gnosis and modern technology. The name derives from the Avestan Fra-Data—an etymological nod to his birth name and the concept of that which is "given forth" or revealed.

His work, Marcion's Evangelion, was born not from academic obsession, but from a direct personal encounter with the Christ consciousness—an experience parallel to the Pauline revelation. Utilizing the analytical rigor of data systems and the generative power of AI, he seeks to surgically separate the "Conscious Universe" (Christ) from the tribal entanglements of the Abrahamic deity. He writes for those seeking the signal amidst centuries of noise.

Connect with the author at:
forthgivenone@gmail.com

[FILE_END_RECORD: 140/2026]
[RECONSTRUCTION_COMPLETE]

www.ingramcontent.com/pod-product-compliance
Lightning Source LLC
LaVergne TN
LVHW090517110826
845146LV00003B/888